OPPORTUNITIES

in

W9-BXT-120

Teaching Careers

OPPORTUNITIES

Teaching Careers

REVISED EDITION

JANET FINE

McGraw·Hill

New York   Chicago   San Francisco   Lisbon   London   Madrid   Mexico City
Milan   New Delhi   San Juan   Seoul   Singapore   Sydney   Toronto

The *McGraw·Hill* Companies

Library of Congress Cataloging-in-Publication Data

Fine, Janet.
    Opportunities in teaching careers / Janet Fine.— Rev. ed.
       p.   cm.
    ISBN 0-07-143817-3
    1. Teaching—Vocational guidance—United States.   I. Title.

    LB1775.2.F55   2005
    371.1′0023—dc22   2004024620

2 3 4 5 6 7 8 9 0   DOC/DOC   0 9 8 7 6

ISBN 0-07-143817-3

Interior design by Rattray Design

McGraw-Hill books are available at special quantity discounts to use as premiums and sales promotions, or for use in corporate training programs. For more information, please write to the Director of Special Sales, Professional Publishing, McGraw-Hill, Two Penn Plaza, New York, NY 10121-2298. Or contact your local bookstore.

BK
*12.42

This book is printed on acid-free paper.

To my mother, Lillian Fine, a teacher who, for the past fifty years, has inspired her students and has found the teaching profession an eternal renewal of new ideas. Her students today are still as eager to learn as she is to teach.

CONTENTS

FOREWORD

To TEACH IS to contribute to society and to our future in very special ways. To teach is to give something to others. To become a teacher is to enter a challenging profession in which the work is hard but the satisfactions can be enormous. Teaching is a service profession with endless opportunities for lifelong learning and intellectual growth in a world of new ideas and constant activity.

There is no more important work and no more important time for you to enter the teaching profession. A growing demand for teachers presents great opportunities to those who will enter the teaching profession during the next decade. An increased nationwide focus on education has made this an ideal time to consider a teaching career. Efforts to reform and improve our educational system have highlighted the importance of the role of the teacher to a far greater extent than ever before. Tangible results of these efforts include increases in teachers' salaries, the strengthening of the teacher's role in schools and school districts, improved training, and increased respect and acknowledgment for their work.

Education and the teaching profession will offer a myriad of opportunities in the coming years. Shortages already exist in particular subject areas and in work with particular groups of students. For example, mathematics and science teachers are needed nationwide; special education teachers are needed to work with at-risk children; minority teachers are needed, especially in urban schools, as their ranks decrease and the number of minority students grows. It is important to note, too, that the need for future generations of scholars to teach in our colleges and universities may also reach alarming proportions.

The essence of teaching is a deep understanding of subject matter and of people. Teachers learn to use this understanding to motivate and to educate those in their charge. Teachers are communicators. They convey what they know and encourage even their youngest students to probe beyond the surface, to question, and to think critically about what they are learning. Good teachers provide opportunities for their students to develop "ways of knowing"—ways of thinking and discovering. They must impart an excitement about learning and must foster students' natural curiosity. To do this, teachers must understand their students as individuals and be familiar with how children and adolescents with diverse backgrounds and abilities develop and learn.

Teachers may work with many different populations, subject areas, and in a wide variety of settings. People of all ages, from infants to the elderly, spend all or part of their days in programs headed by teachers. Areas include early childhood education, day care, elementary education, secondary education (high school), special education, college teaching, and teaching special populations. In addition, there are many related areas, including school psychology, speech therapy, guidance counseling, and educational administration.

Opportunities in Teaching Careers, by Janet Fine, includes a wealth of practical information for anyone who is considering teaching from the elementary school to the college level. One can discover much about the history, current situation, and future prospects in the teaching field as well as some related fields. Included are many references and suggestions about where to find specific information on financial support, making occupational choices, and other relevant matters.

Teaching offers many opportunities for your future. The exciting challenges include incorporating new developments of technology into education and addressing the many problems related to health, family, and community issues. If you become a teacher, you choose a career that offers the personal satisfaction of knowing you will make a difference in America's future.

Judith Berman Brandenburg
Former Dean of Teachers College
Columbia University

1

Overview of the Teaching Field

Teaching developed from scholars such as Aristotle, Socrates, and other philosophers in ancient Greece. The rich academic atmosphere of ancient Athens and other Greek cities contributed to a fostering of knowledge. Education also flourished in ancient China, where wandering sages of the Orient made important contributions to art and science. In Africa, the universities of Sangkore and Timbuktu were important and revered seats of learning.

Schools in Europe first grew up around churches and monasteries. The Renaissance helped open doors of learning to larger numbers of people by showing new paths to the education of the mind and spirit.

Teaching as we know it today was not at first a well-respected profession in the United States. Teaching was regarded as merely a part-time pursuit leading into another occupation. Very few people made teaching a life career; in many areas, clergymen served as both teachers and religious leaders.

Even at the beginning of the 1900s, American teachers still gained little respect or money, and many were ill-prepared. As Marshall Donlevy noted in his book *Power to the Teacher*, a teacher was expected to be cheerful, meek, loyal, and, most of all, quiet. When a superintendent of schools in New York was asked in 1905 if there were any conditions to justify a teacher's complaints about a superior, he replied, "Absolutely none."

Teaching was not thought of as a profession by many. In 1906, Fassett Cotton, Indiana state superintendent of public instruction, expressed similar doubts in the fiftieth-anniversary volume of the National Education Association. He said:

> After all, one of the greatest causes of poor pay to teachers is the fact that the vast majority of teachers are not professional educators. The calling is still a stepping-stone to other professions. . . . The prospective lawyer, doctor or minister [is] willing to take temporary employment as a teacher at a lower salary than a professional educator can afford to take. . . . Many are teaching because they had not the profession of their choice. Poverty makes teachers subservient to society. They get used to small means and small ways, and for this reason are incapacitated for the big things in life.

It was not until the 1830s that education and teaching began to assume the professional character that it has today. From about 1836 until the end of the Civil War, industrialization tightened its grip on what had formerly been a rural society. Each year U.S. cities grew, swelled both by migrating farm workers and increasing numbers of immigrants. The new common schools founded in American cities proved indispensable in helping huge waves of immigrants prepare for citizenship and enabling them to share in and contribute to the spectacular economic growth of the United States.

A growing awareness that education was the main support of democracy helped spark an educational awakening in this country.

American public schools were established and faced with the problem of how to create the educated citizenry needed for an industrialized society. In the words of Horace Mann, one of the first great American advocates of public education, "The object of the common school is to give every child a free, straight, solid pathway by which he can walk directly up from the ignorance of an infant to a knowledge of the primary duties of a man."

What did these developments mean for the teacher? Teaching became a stabilized profession. It took its place alongside the older established professions of law, medicine, and the clergy. Normal schools were set up to provide specialized training for teachers. State and county supervision of schools was established, creating a greater unity among teachers and a greatly improved educational program. Examinations were developed for certifying and licensing professional teachers. A graded system of schools did away with loosely structured colonial schoolrooms.

In short, teaching became an organized profession with a definite status and prestige in our national life and in the community. High schools and vocational schools were founded, guidance counseling was developed, and school sports and extracurricular activities were established as valuable links to classroom learning. Perhaps the biggest boons to education were the development of instructional materials and the improvement of courses of study that extended the instructional value of textbooks. Also significant was the lengthening of the school year, especially in the cities, making teaching a full-time job.

At first, men dominated the teaching profession. Then came the growing role of the female teacher. There were three reasons for the increase in the number of female teachers: first, there was a growing demand for teachers as the population doubled and tripled during the 1800s; second, the Civil War called male teachers to the battlefield; and finally, there was greater economy in employing women, because women were usually paid less than men. With few other alternatives for careers, women flooded the teaching field, making the profession a predominantly female occupation.

Strict rules fostered negative stereotypes about female teachers. For many years, female teachers were permitted no dancing, no makeup, no bobbed hair, no marriage, and no companionship with the opposite sex in public. Rules were enforced, and they penetrated the teachers' personal lives. As recently as 1935, this rule remained in one county school system's books: "Any conduct such as staying out late at night, which might cause criticism of the teacher, will not be tolerated by the school board."

According to 1971 research from the Organization for Economic Cooperation and Development, many women left schools immediately after getting married or becoming pregnant. This attrition had a direct effect on the supply and demand of teachers in the school system. In a 1961 poll, 84 percent of the women said they had left teaching before retirement, citing marriage as their main reason.

As times changed, many women regarded teaching as the perfect profession because the hours and vacations made it possible for them to spend more time with their families. But currently all stereotypes of the female teacher have been shattered by a new breed of committed women, single or married, who have decided to make teaching their full-time career.

The number of men in teaching has shifted in recent years. In 1958 and 1959, for the first time since the U.S. Office of Education started collecting data on teachers in 1890, male teachers outnumbered female teachers in the nation's high schools (52.2 percent to 47.8 percent). By 1980, the number of single female college students (ages eighteen through twenty-four) for the first time equaled that of male students. By 1990, female teachers had increased in certain areas to outnumber their male colleagues, and in 2001, they far outnumbered male teachers in public schools (79 percent to 21 percent), although more senior high school teachers were male than were middle and elementary school teachers (43 percent to 25 percent versus 9 percent) according to a report called *Status of the American Public School Teacher 2000–2001*, by the National Education Association. Males comprised 25.1 percent of U.S. public school teachers in 2003. Interestingly, the Southeast has had smaller percentages of male teachers than all other regions in every survey taken from 1966 to 2003; states such as Indiana, Massachusetts, Kansas, and Oregon have had higher percentages of male teachers.

According to this same report, even the percentage of bachelor's degrees awarded to women and men was equalized by 2001. The report also found that from 1966 to 2001, the percentage of teachers receiving their degrees from public institutions increased from 71 percent in 1966 to 77 percent in 2001. Those teachers with six-year diplomas and master's degrees reached an all-time high of 86 percent in 1981, declining to 78 percent in 1996, and reported at 56 percent of all teachers in 2001.

The Profession Today

"The good teacher believes in the subject and is genuinely, unashamedly enthusiastic about it," declares Gilbert Highet in the book *Teaching—The Immortal Profession: The Joys of Teaching and Learning*. The good teacher can stimulate and help improve the minds and lives of countless students by sharing with them the gift of knowledge. This is the true challenge of teaching today. The teaching profession offers great opportunities for qualified men and women ready to meet this challenge.

"Kids are and always will be what great teachers live for," concluded a report about award-winning first-year teachers. "Their smiles are an antidote to a bad day, and their progress is an unending source of satisfaction," said many of the teachers.

Remembering that a commitment to the learning process of a child will shape the child's future is one of the greatest motivations to become a teacher. The Metropolitan Life Survey of the American Teacher conducted a poll of the experiences of one thousand new public school teachers, finding that the most important concern was in the teaching procedure.

"Teaching is an awesome responsibility with many rewards," commented Kathleen Mellon, 2004 Teacher of the Year, at the National Education Association (NEA) convention. She teaches English as a Second Language (ESL) in North Kingston, Rhode Island, and was given the award by the NEA for "exemplifying how teachers are helping diverse students attain their dreams."

"Life provides few opportunities to affect the world," she said. "However, the connections teachers and students make provide the chance to make a profound difference."

The role of the teacher, as never before, is being closely scrutinized to ensure that the future generation of Americans will be absorbing the basic tenets of education. When the National Commission on Excellence in Education published the report *A Nation at Risk* in 1983, it recommended steps to "stem the rising tide of mediocrity" in primary schools and improve conditions for teachers to achieve this goal. A second report, *America's Teachers Ten Years After a Nation at Risk*, examined the changes that had occurred in the teaching occupation up until the mid-1990s.

A report called *The Status of Teaching as a Profession* further delved into the professionalism of the workplace of elementary and secondary school teachers, saying it could make a greater impact with the teacher's commitment to the profession. According to the report, "proponents of teacher professionalization have argued that improvements in the commitment of teachers is one of the outcomes most likely to be affected by new teacher reform efforts."

State of Technology

"We are concerned about the state of technology programs for the nation's teachers," said Arthur Wise, president of the National Council for Accreditation of Teacher Education (NCATE), a Washington, D.C.–based coalition of thirty organizations that sets standards for education schools and accredits about five hundred institutions.

According to its report, *Technology and the New Professional Teacher: Preparing for the Twenty-First-Century Classroom,* guidelines set in 1995 incorporated technology into teacher preparation programs. These guidelines were once more revamped in 2000 and are adopting these suggestions to the technological age of the Internet, distance learning, and the new skills of the twenty-first century shaping the future. What is now being called the Digital Age, which started in 2000, incorporates some innovative digital cameras and equipment so that teacher and student merge learning through a machine.

Some of the change for the accreditation process and in the schools, according to the report, recommends stimulating effective use of technology in teacher education, which will improve the current accreditation process and help institutions prepare new teachers for technology in their classrooms.

The National Coalition for Technology in Education and Training (NCTET), a nonpartisan coalition of education organizations and technology companies, offers suggestions how to best contact candidates and demonstrates the effectiveness of technology in raising student achievement. "Although recent efforts have significantly raised the level of technology access in our schools," said NCET board member Barbara Stein, "many classrooms still appear to be relics of previous eras. All of our students deserve access to the tools that will help them succeed in this century."

Yet, in the twenty-first century, schools are finding that although they are progressing in technology, basic writing and reading skills have lagged behind. One 1975 literacy study concluded that roughly twenty-five million American adults were illiterate. Years later, these numbers have only worsened. Many of the people in America cannot read or write. A 1998 survey found that almost one-fourth of the students in America do not have proper writing and reading skills, and the National Assessment of Educational Progress's (NAEP) Nation's Report Card, which in 2002 surveyed the reading and writing performance of fourth-, eighth-, and twelfth-grade students around the country, concluded that students in stable families and better schools exceeded performance expectations in reading and writing.

The report said that with the ever-increasing immigrant population in the United States, the need for strong English skills is growing. Several government incentives have been allocated to encourage literacy as part of the No Child Left Behind Act of 2001, including Reading First, a fund for reading instruction material for children in kindergarten through grade three; Even Start Family Literacy, which provides funds to help integrate early childhood education with literacy; and Migrant Education, financial assistance to improve education for migrant children.

More Jobs

In spite of the problems teachers face, why are so many people attracted to the teaching field? According to U.S. government statistics, teaching is the largest single profession in America. Thousands teach part-time in schools and in vocational training centers. Many more work as superintendents, principals, and supervisors. Still others teach in preschools and adult education and recreation programs. An estimated 3.8 million people work as administrative, professional, and support staff at all levels of education.

Changes in the number of staff employed in education institutions reflect trends in enrollment; changes in the economy; and specific state, local, and national program priorities, according to a report called *Rankings and Estimates 2003 and 2004*, by the National Education Association. There were 3,035,249 classroom teachers in 2002–03 with a slight increase in 2003–04, proving the pundits wrong about an "oversupply" of teachers in the 1970s. Some areas, in fact, are now experiencing teacher shortages.

In fall 2002, U.S. public school enrollment was 47.8 million students, up 0.9 percent over fall 2001, and it increased to 48.2 million students in 2003–04. Public enrollment for prekindergarten through grade twelve is projected to increase to an all-time high of 49.7 million by 2013. The largest enrollment increases were in the states of Nevada, Arizona, Texas, and Michigan, with seventeen states and the District of Columbia experiencing the greatest declines including South Carolina, Vermont, and North Dakota.

A Teacher's Role

Each teacher has her or his own definition of the teacher's role. Perhaps the most obvious and most important aspect of a teacher's role is to encourage learning. A 1987 reappraisal of the 1960 Master Plan for Higher Education in California—often used as a model for other states—recommended that teaching skills be a greater consideration for tenure or promotion than research accomplishments. Students should be encouraged to "learn in the classroom" from teachers dedicated to teaching. Now, in the early millennium years, this model has been reinforced with programs to increase high-quality teaching preparation and practice.

When more than twelve thousand students were asked in a 1950s poll to submit letters on "The Teacher Who Has Helped Me Most," the best teachers, according to students, were those who "seek teaching as a career and a profession."

Instilling in students the desire for knowledge contributes to the profound influence of teachers. An appreciation of life begins with a joy of learning. As Aristotle observed, "All who have meditated on the art of governing mankind have been convinced that the fate of empires depends on the education of youth."

The Need for Qualified Teachers

Changes occurring in the academic marketplace have affected teacher supply and demand. The decade of the 1970s recorded a change for elementary and secondary school teachers. New teachers faced a tight labor market, and many could not find teaching jobs. As the post–World War II baby boom leveled off, many young men and women did not enter teacher training, believing that the supply of teachers would far exceed the demand.

According to the National Education Association (NEA), teaching areas in which the supply of teachers is least adequate include mathematics, natural and physical sciences, computer training, distributive education, industrial arts, and agriculture. The NEA's report *Rankings and Estimates 2003 and 2004* estimated the number of classroom teachers in public and private elementary and secondary schools increasing from 3.35 million in 2002–03 to an estimated 3.51 million in 2003–04. (See Table 1.1.)

According to estimates for 2003–04, the small increase in instructional staff over the previous year represents a decline in elementary teachers and an increase in secondary teachers. (See

Table 1.2.) Since 1993–94, the number of secondary school teachers increased 29.3 percent. Schools needed to hire 2.2 million teachers during the following decade.

Table 1.1 Ten-Year Trend in Total Number of Classroom Teachers, 1994–2004

| School Year | Classroom Teachers | | Total |
	Elementary School	Secondary School	
1993–94	1,517,357	994,823	2,512,180
1994–95	1,517,239	1,048,157	2,565,396
1995–96	1,542,899	1,061,803	2,604,702
1996–97	1,585,672	1,085,651	2,671,323
1997–98	1,630,026	1,115,733	2,745,759
1998–99	1,649,528	1,164,104	2,813,632
1999–2000	1,696,359	1,194,712	2,891,071
2000–2001	1,727,020	1,214,248	2,941,268
2001–02	1,744,617	1,239,758	2,984,375
2002–03	1,771,515	1,263,734	3,035,249
2003–04	1,764,977	1,286,753	3,051,730

Source: *Rankings and Estimates: Rankings of the States 2003 and Estimates of School Statistics 2004*, National Education Association, 2004.

Table 1.2 Ten-Year Trend in Total Instructional Staff, 1994–2004

| School Year | Instructional Staff | Percent Change | |
		From 1993–94	From Previous Year
1993–94	2,865,042	—	1.9
1994–95	2,919,258	1.9	1.9
1995–96	2,960,203	3.3	1.4
1996–97	3,030,715	5.8	2.4
1997–98	3,110,044	8.6	2.6
1998–99	3,184,550	11.2	2.4
1999–2000	3,272,539	14.2	2.8
2000–2001	3,333,526	16.4	1.9
2001–02	3,385,567	18.2	1.6
2002–03	3,449,584	20.4	1.9
2003–04	3,468,933	21.1	0.6

Source: *Rankings and Estimates: Rankings of the States 2003 and Estimates of School Statistics 2004*, National Education Association, 2004.

Workplace

Redesigning the workplace so that innovation and improvement are built into classroom daily activities is one of the issues that will be vital in the teaching profession.

"The current school organization is an anachronism. It was designed for an earlier period for conditions that no longer hold. It constrains the creation of a new profession of teaching that is so badly needed," writes Michael Fullan in the book *The Meaning of Educational Change*. He implores professionals to "take responsibility for empowering themselves and others through becoming experts in the change process."

Math Teachers: Shortage and Solution

The area of mathematics has experienced the severest teacher shortage of any subject, according to findings by the Association of School, College, and University Staffing. For example, in 1998, New York City recruited twenty-three math and science teachers from Austria to fill available positions. One major problem confronting math and science teachers at the secondary and even elementary levels is the lure of business. But more students are studying mathematics, according to National Center for Education Statistics 2004 findings, with the percentage of high school students who had completed advanced courses in mathematics from the early 1980s until 2000 increasing from 26 to 45 percent.

Several incentives for teachers of math and science for staying in the profession have been proposed throughout the United States. Beginning salaries for teachers are much less than those in computer science and business, although schools have begun to raise salaries and offer special perks such as mortgage loans, special retirement packages, and other benefits not offered by business.

The engineering faculty positions in U.S. schools are also recording a 10 percent vacancy rate. The demand for scientists and engineers rose rapidly in the 1990s and early 2000s in both industry and academia, according to a report from the National Science Foundation. The report predicted that under these circumstances, "the academic sector will experience the brunt of any shortage," because colleges and universities cannot win bidding wars with industry.

New Incentives

Industry has also been urged to participate in building up strong science, engineering, and mathematics faculties. Some suggestions include direct industry financial support in the form of scholarships, direct grants to the schools, and stipends that would make salaries of teachers competitive with market salaries. For example, Columbia University's microelectronics science lab, which is also home to the Center for Telecommunications Research, is an $8-million-a-year activity funded in part by the National Science Foundation and created to encourage students to stay in the science and engineering academic area and produce important research results while they are going to college.

"Expanding cooperative programs in which industry shares its personnel with schools is a way to keep good people in the teaching profession," says mathematics professor Dr. James Vick. "We must avoid the pillaging effect of industry on the intelligent and productive teachers that we need in our secondary schools."

One innovative way to increase interaction with business and education is the establishment of special programs for leading businesspeople, bringing them back into the classroom.

Harvard Business School yearly accepts industrialists from around the world to a month-long program of ·classes. "Better teaching means better job achievement," says one participant at his yearly "schooling." "Business schools must look at ethics; it is a moral responsibility to deal with business ethics in [the] curriculum to help guide the moral fibre for business in the future."

Business School Brain Drain

According to the American Assembly of Collegiate Schools of Business (AACSB), 16 percent of tenure-track teaching positions in business schools—full-time positions almost always filled by Ph.D.s—were unfilled in 1987. This was the highest vacancy rate ever, with 22 percent in accounting and 26 percent in management information systems. Additionally, during the 1990s through 2004 many professors retired, causing a "business school brain drain." The demand for business professors has outstripped supply. About 40 percent of entering doctoral students in business programs at accredited American universities were foreign—double the percentage a decade ago. Many of these foreign students will not legally be able to teach in the United States.

Business schools are increasing salaries and incentives in a move to compete with industry. Major corporations are also contributing to student training with such programs as the National Doctoral Fellowship Program, which provides a stipend plus tuition for selected students going for a doctoral degree in business. Many of these corporations say that their aim is not to hire the Ph.D.s but rather to turn them into better professors.

Supply and Demand

According to Department of Labor 2003 findings, job opportunities for teachers will vary from average to stable depending on the locality, grade level, and subject taught. Overall student enrollments, a key factor in the demand for teachers, is projected to rise more slowly than in the past through 2012. Job openings are expected with the retirement of a large number of teachers and a higher rate of turnover among beginning teachers. The supply of teachers is expected to increase in response to reports of improved job prospects, better pay, more teacher involvement in school policy, and greater public interest in education. Various states are implementing policies that will encourage more students to become teachers.

Degrees Given

In recent years, the total number of bachelor's and master's degrees granted in education has increased steadily, according to the National Center for Education Statistics Report *The Condition of Education 2004*, which projected a new high of students each year from 2004 to 2013. (See Figure 1.1.) Another interesting trend is the prediction that in the next ten years, full-time undergraduate enrollment is expected to increase at a faster rate than part-time enrollment. More teachers may be drawn from a reserve pool of career changers, substitute teachers, and teachers completing alternative certification programs. Competition for qualified teachers among some localities will likely continue, with schools luring teachers from other states and districts with bonuses and higher pay.

As the children of the baby-boom generation get older, smaller numbers of young children will enter schools, resulting in average employment growth for all teachers, from preschool through secondary grades. Projected enrollments vary by geographical school region from the fast-growing states in the South and West—particularly California, Texas, Georgia, Florida, Idaho, Hawaii, Alaska, and New Mexico—with larger enrollment increases, to enrollments

Figure 1.1 Undergraduate Enrollment

Undergraduate Enrollment: Total undergraduate enrollment in degree-granting two- and four-year postsecondary institutions (in thousands), by sex, attendance status, and type of institution, with projections: Fall 1970–2013

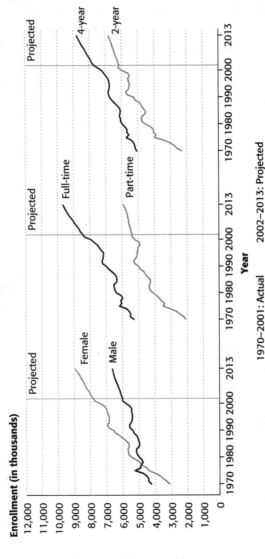

Source: U.S. Department of Education, NCES, *The Condition of Education 2004,* June 2004.

in the Northeast and Midwest, which are expected to hold relatively steady or to decline.

Subject Matter

The job market for teachers also continues to vary by subject taught. Many inner-city schools and rural and remote education districts offer relatively low salaries and have difficulty attracting and retaining enough teachers, so job prospects should be better in these areas than in suburban districts. Many private and federal teaching programs are targeting these schools for beginning teachers.

Reports find that many school districts have difficulty hiring qualified teachers in some subject areas—mathematics, science (especially chemistry and physics), bilingual education, and foreign languages. Qualified vocational teachers, at both middle school and secondary school levels, also are in demand in a variety of fields, including general elementary education, physical education, and social studies. Increasing enrollments of minorities, coupled with a shortage of minority teachers, would encourage recruitment of minority teachers and a greater demand for bilingual teachers and for those who teach English as a second language. At the federal level, legislation that is likely to affect teachers, such as the No Child Left Behind Act, has an emphasis on schools hiring and retaining only qualified teachers, which may lead to an increase in funding for schools that currently lack such teachers.

Teacher Shortages in the United States

Articles appearing in the American publication *Phi Delta Kappan* reported the following information on the teacher supply and demand situation in the United States.

- The government projects a 21 percent growth in demand for teachers, librarians, and counselors from 1996 to 2006.
- Growth in demand is projected to be largest for special education teachers, with a forecasted increase of 59 percent over the decade ending in 2006.
- The demand for elementary teachers is projected to increase by 20 percent from 1996 to 2006, compared to 10 percent for preschool or kindergarten teachers.
- Growth in demand for secondary teachers, primarily in math and science, is projected to be 22 percent from 1996 to 2006.
- The National Center for Education Statistics projects that the teacher attrition rate in U.S. public schools will be 7 percent from 2000 to 2010.
- At least half of the teacher attrition rate is expected to be accounted for by teachers who are retiring and those finding employment outside of education.
- About 22 percent of all newly hired teachers are typically gone from the classroom within three years, and 50 percent of newly hired teachers in urban areas are gone within the same time period.

The National Commission on Teaching and America's Future report *No Dream Denied* found that the "root of the teacher shortage is in fact a severe teacher retention problem." The report established that almost a third of new teachers leave the classroom after three years and that close to 50 percent leave after five years. Additionally for every one teacher who retires, there are three teachers who leave for other reasons.

Here are some examples of the teacher supply and demand situation in certain states and the efforts being made to deal with teacher shortages, as reported in education statistics from the National Education Association.

California

- The number of teachers to be hired in the 2000s is projected to be between 260,000 and 300,000.
- Entrance into the teaching force will be made easier for those who have degrees but no teaching credentials and for those who have not completed their degrees.
- More than twenty-nine thousand teachers are estimated to be currently teaching with an emergency credential.
- The state university system is working on an intensive immersion program to shorten the course work required to obtain a teaching credential from two years to one year.
- Loan forgiveness is being increased for math and science teachers willing to teach in inner city or rural areas.

Maryland

- Free rent for a month, low-interest loans, and tuition reimbursement are being offered in some counties to attract new teachers.
- Only 57 percent of teachers hired in Prince George County were fully certified in their teaching areas.
- Recruiters in Prince George County travel to job fairs on the East Coast and throughout the South.
- Newly hired special education teachers in Baltimore were moved up on the salary schedule as if they had taught for four years.
- Maryland's state superintendent has proposed the use of tax credits for new teachers.

- Some members of the state legislature are discussing the possibility of implementing a differential pay schedule providing higher pay to teachers in high-need subject areas.

New York
- Recruiters in New York City hired twenty-three math and science teachers from Austria to fill available positions.

Texas
- In Dallas and Fort Worth, signing bonuses of $500 to $2,000 are being offered.
- In El Paso, $2,000 signing bonuses are being offered to math teachers.

The National Commission on Teaching and America's Future, a private organization, has found that Midwestern states such as Minnesota and Wisconsin, with a slower population growth, are not experiencing the same teacher shortages as Texas.

Such sophisticated methods of recruitment as videoconferencing, job fairs, and bonuses and relocation fees have been initiated by schools seeking to compete with private companies that offer higher salaries. Math, special education, and bilingual education have been reported as areas with maximum shortages.

Programs Encouraging New Teachers

New York City's Teaching Fellows and Teach for America are encouraging students to enter the teaching arena after college to gain experience.

New York City's Teaching Fellows was started in 2000 to recruit teachers in high-need New York City schools with severe teacher shortages. To join, a bachelor's degree is required and candidates receive two months of preservice training during the summer before they enter the classroom. The preservice training includes course work toward earning a master's in education; field-based work with experienced New York City teachers; and meetings with an advisor to learn teaching skills and classroom-management techniques. A $2,500 stipend is given to the student during the summer and upon completion of the preservice training.

Teaching Fellows enter the classroom as full-time first-year teachers with a bachelor's or master's degree in the subject they teach. The city pays most of the cost for Teaching Fellows to pursue a master's in education in the evenings and on weekends at one of fourteen area colleges with which the program has partnered. After three years of teaching, they can apply for the state's professional certification. The Fellows accept about two thousand candidates from an array of fields. The program received twenty thousand applications for the 2003–04 year. For more information on the New York City's Teaching Fellows program, visit its website nycteachingfellows.org.

"I'm not sure I would be a teacher for the rest of my life, but joining New York City's Teaching Fellows program after graduating from the University of Berkeley is providing me a chance to see how I will do as a teacher," said Mara Nerenberg. "I don't have an education background, but this provides a good opportunity to teach in the inner schools of New York and really get experience and do something positive after graduation."

Another organization providing teaching opportunities is the national service network of Teach for America, started in 1990 and designed for recent college graduates to attract a "new pool of people into teaching." Incorporated by Congress as the AmeriCorps, it is based in thirteen sites around the country with five hundred students selected annually. Applicants must have bachelor's degrees, but there is no previous education course work required. After undergoing a five-week training course, students must be willing to relocate and teach for two years at school districts that face a shortage of qualified and certified teachers in specialized subjects.

Teach for America corps members are paid directly by the school districts with salaries ranging from $33,500 in urban regions to $20,000 in rural regions and an education reward of $4,725 toward financial loans or future tuition. Several of the local offices have established partnerships with universities to facilitate teaching certification.

As stated by Teach for America, the program is to encourage "those who may not have considered teaching, but who will help meet students' immediate needs in urban and rural areas and go on to be advocates for quality education."

Retirement Programs

New retirement packages have been offered to teachers in the past few years. Some states, like Texas, have now offered retired teachers jobs with their pensions remaining, and that might signify a trend. Each state varies in its benefits, and the Teachers Insurance and Annuity Association-College Retirement Equities Fund (TIAA-CREF) is being advocated for public school teachers. As many states are now in need of teachers, those who move to new employment in other states will be negotiating their contracts to keep the credits accrued toward retirement.

Good Teachers Wanted

Many countries in addition to the United States have reported being unable to meet their teacher demand. The Organization for

Economic Cooperation and Development (OECD) reports that many schools said they were forced to lower hiring standards to meet their needs.

The OECD survey of schools tried to make an international comparison of how different countries struggle to overcome the shortage of teaching staff. Countries have chosen different ways to fill teaching vacancies. Danish school authorities, for example, prefer teachers working overtime, while in Austria, educators report a preference for a high pupil/class ratio. In some parts of the United States, it has sometimes been necessary to shorten the school year because of the small number of teachers.

The tendency to crowd classes, work teachers overtime, and lessen personal teacher contact is a situation that teachers, parents, and students are fighting. Teachers have been making front-page news with strikes and work stoppages, demanding better conditions in the schools. A trend of militancy has developed among many teachers who, after struggling to achieve a high level of education and proficiency in their profession, are hampered by the poor conditions encountered in the schools.

Specialists

Changes in curricula and in the needs of society have created demands for certain types of teachers. As students become more career-minded, schools are orienting more classes to specific subjects. Long gone are the days when many students will be content to study philosophy, history, and art for four years of school. The increasingly competitive job market now calls for specialization.

New and expanded school programs have been established, often with federal assistance. There is a need for many more teachers in early childhood education, teachers especially prepared to work effectively with disadvantaged students, reading specialists, remedial teachers of various kinds, guidance counselors, and other specialists.

Sources of Information About Teacher Supply and Demand

Those who want to keep up with changing developments in teacher supply and demand will discover that the latest editions of the reports on teacher supply and demand produced by the research division of the National Education Association are most useful. The Department of Labor and U.S. Department of Education also issue annual statistics. On an international scale, the OECD books and surveys of schools around the world are helpful.

University placement services supply much of the information for these reports. One such center, the Education Placement Services at the University of Texas, finds jobs for qualified teachers at Texas community colleges. Other sources, including private foundation studies, industry findings, and education surveys, all help to pinpoint specific teacher supply and demand information.

The Department of Education and other authorities predict that more kindergarten, elementary, secondary, and college and university teaching jobs will be available due to the increase in the nation's birth rate and the retirement of a large number of teachers in the next few years. Levels of public school enrollment anticipated during the 2003–04 school year represents the seventeenth consecutive increase since 1986–87. A Carnegie Foundation report said that an estimated four hundred thousand to five hundred thousand faculty openings will occur over the next twenty years. This trend is resulting in younger and younger teachers due to the retirement of the veteran teachers and those opting for early retirement.

Private schools occupy a marginal but increasingly important part of government involvement, with the prediction of more enrollment in non-Catholic private schools.

Since the early 1990s, according to *Rankings and Estimates 2003 and 2004*, both the school age and sixty-five-and-over populations have been increasing in numbers, with education and health care in competition for public funding. There was a 0.6 percent increase from 2000–2003 to 2003–04 in instructional staff of a district or school—comprising classroom teachers, principals, supervisors, librarians, guidance and psychological personnel, and related instructional workers—although a decline in elementary teachers (−0.4) and an increase in secondary teachers (1.8). The elementary school classroom teachers experienced a net increase of 16.3 percent since 1993–94, and secondary school teachers increased 29.3 percent in the same ten-year period.

Projected employment for teachers in preschool through grade twelve, including special education in 2002 through 2012, according to the *Occupational Outlook Quarterly* 2004, will be 12.53 million with a 20 percent change reflecting an increased annual employment. (See Table 1.3.)

The Rewards of Teaching

Most educators agree that the greatest reward of teaching comes from the students. Helping children grow and learn is indeed satisfying. In addition, teachers keep abreast of new ideas, new books, and new trends in learning. Although teaching methods and conditions vary from state to state, there are some aspects of teaching that nearly all districts have in common.

In the booklet *Teaching as a Career*, produced by the American Federation of Teachers, teachers reported on how their job security

Table 1.3 Employment of Wage and Salary Workers in Educational Services by Occupation, 2002, and Projected Change, 2002–12 (Employment in Thousands)

Occupation	Employment, 2002		Percent Change, 2002–12
	Number	*Percent*	
All occupations	12,527	100.0	19.9
Management, business, and financial occupations	825	6.6	23.0
Education administrators, elementary and secondary school	204	1.6	21.4
Education administrators, postsecondary	120	1.0	26.9
Professional and related occupations	8,210	65.5	23.9
Computer support specialists	56	0.4	18.6
Clinical, counseling, and school psychologists	43	0.3	19.0
Educational, vocational, and school counselors	177	1.4	13.7
Child, family, and school social workers	36	0.3	19.1
Postsecondary teachers	1,512	12.1	38.3
Preschool teachers, except special education	67	0.5	27.0
Kindergarten teachers, except special education	154	1.2	28.3
Elementary school teachers, except special education	1,427	11.4	14.9
Middle school teachers, except special and vocational education	580	4.6	8.8
Secondary school teachers, except special and vocational education	982	7.8	18.1
Vocational education teachers, secondary school	102	0.8	9.3
Special education teachers, preschool, kindergarten, and elementary school	203	1.6	30.4
Special education teachers, middle school	86	0.7	30.5
Special education teachers, secondary school	131	1.0	30.3
Adult literacy, remedial education, and GED teachers and instructors	49	0.4	24.6

Self-enrichment education teachers	80	0.6	53.5
All other teachers—primary, secondary, and adult	425	3.4	43.1
Librarians	94	0.7	6.4
Library technicians	54	0.4	20.9
Instructional coordinators	68	0.5	27.9
Teacher assistants	1,047	8.4	21.9

Source: *Occupational Outlook Handbook 2004–05*, Bureau of Labor Statistics, 2004.

compared to that of other workers. Four out of five states have tenure laws, wherein after two or three years of employment a teacher cannot be fired without good cause. Teachers who are incompetent, however, can be dismissed. In the past, teachers were often fired because of a principal's gripe, because they became involved in politics, or, in the case of female teachers, because they married.

In addition to this measure of job security, teaching offers a uniform salary schedule. Earnings are based on years of experience and training. Teaching offers fringe benefits that usually include health insurance, paid sick leave, and a retirement plan. Teachers are also able to use the summer months for study or travel.

Median annual earnings of kindergarten, elementary, middle, and secondary school teachers ranged from $39,810 to $44,340 in 2002–03; the lowest 10 percent earned $24,960 to $29,850; the top 10 percent earned $62,890 to $68,530. Median earnings for preschool teachers were $19,270, according to the American Federation of Teachers. Private school teachers generally earn less than public school teachers. Over the decade from 1993 to 2003, average salaries for public school teachers increased 2.6 percent.

New opportunities in teaching are increasing as society itself changes. There are more jobs in teaching English as a second language and in language programs, the computer field, adult education, film and video, and other expanding areas that need more specialization.

The international prospects of obtaining a teaching job are also excellent. A teacher can often choose a country and teach there. Teachers can also study in foreign universities and receive credit and support for these studies.

Perhaps the greatest return to be expected is the joy of watching students learn and progress. "In their formative years it is my job to show children it is beautiful to learn," says Lillian Echevarria, a Miami, Florida, kindergarten teacher. "With the little ones, anything they learn, you know you taught it," she continues. "You get them first, before anyone, and you can really see them learn. This is why I keep on teaching, why I love it."

Qualities of a Good Teacher

Whether you decide to teach in the elementary grades, in high school, or in college, there are certain basic personal qualities you should have if you want to be successful in your job. How you answer these questions will give you valuable insight into your potential to be a good teacher:

- Do you enjoy good physical and emotional health?
- Do you enjoy working with other people—children, adolescents, adults?
- Do you like to study? (In college teaching this is a must, because your chances for advancement will depend upon your capacity for independent research.)
- Do you become enthusiastic about new ideas, and do you like to discuss them with others?

- How well do you express yourself and explain things to others?
- Do you have a sense of humor?
- Are you interested in what happens in your community, in your city, in your nation, and in the rest of the world?

Every great teacher since Socrates knows that you learn through questioning. If you are a good teacher, you will get your students to respond to you. As a good teacher, you will need enthusiasm, a love of learning, and what former Harvard president James Bryant Conant called "the passion to learn and to understand."

The good teacher treats each child as an individual ready to gain inspiration as well as knowledge. The good teacher is willing to explore the unknown, seeking to contribute new knowledge about the nature of the universe itself. By preserving the best values of the past, a good teacher can make the future a better place in which to live.

The Importance of Personality

The teacher's personality is vital to making school a good experience. When a radio program conducted a poll in which thousands of children were asked to write about the teacher who had been most helpful to them, letter after letter indicated that it was the qualities of the teacher's character that meant more to the student than the subject matter that was taught.

The best teachers were given high ratings in cooperation, democratic spirit, kindness, consideration for the individual pupil, patience, wide interests, personal appearance, fairness, sense of humor, interest in students' problems, and disposition. An interesting note: at the very end of the list was "skill in presenting the subject matter."

A teacher possessing all of these traits will have no trouble providing a healthy, secure atmosphere for his or her class—an atmosphere suited to learning.

Some teachers are so popular, like Principal Saul Bruckner of the Edward Murrow High School in Brooklyn, New York, that students entered a lottery to attend his American history class. Mr. Bruckner's keen wit and innovative methods of teaching were why students wanted to be in his class, despite homework and paper requirements. "In this class, you are appealing to kids on the two things they find most difficult, language and abstraction," says Mr. Bruckner.

It is sometimes said that good teachers are those who have a natural ability for teaching. Yet often a teaching-preparation institution screens teachers for their practical knowledge rather than their instinct for teaching. Demonstrated success in working with students is essential for a good teacher. Many teachers never realize that they do not have teaching ability until they begin to practice teaching. To avoid such a situation, early exploratory experience in working with students is provided in high schools by the Future Teachers of America programs and early in college programs through different societies.

Teacher as a Leader

When the Department of Education hosted the fourth National Teach Forum in 1996, it invited 120 public and private school teachers to Washington, D.C., to explore such questions as: "Why is teacher leadership needed?" "What forms can teacher leadership take?" and "What steps can teachers take to become effective leaders?"

The following "Steps to Develop a Teacher's Progress" were formulated by the forum:

- Participating in professional teacher organizations
- Taking part in school decisions
- Defining what students need to know and need to be able to do
- Sharing ideas with colleagues
- Being a mentor to new teachers
- Helping to make personal decisions
- Improving facilities and technology
- Working with parents
- Creating partnerships with the community
- Creating partnerships with businesses and organizations
- Creating partnerships with colleges and universities to prepare future teachers
- Becoming leaders in the community
- Becoming politically involved
- Leading efforts to make teachers more visible and communicate positive information

The Competent Teacher

Teachers are often viewed as competent if they are living up to the standards the school has established. Keeping up with the competition by publishing the required papers or lecturing on different panels does make a teacher better known but does not make a better teacher. Arthur Combs wrote in the essay *The Personal Approach to Good Teaching*, "If we know what the expert teachers do, or are like, then we can teach the beginners to be like that."

According to Combs, many investigations on the competency of a good teacher have been made, but basic results show that good teaching cannot be defined simply in terms of any particular trait. One study demonstrated that a number of general classes of behavior seemed to be characteristic of good teachers.

"The creation of long lists of competencies is likely to be deeply discouraging and disillusioning to the young teacher," says Combs. "Evaluations of 'goodness' or 'badness' become attached to method, and students thereafter are expected to judge their own adequacies in these terms. The net effect is to set such impossible goals of excellence that no one can ever hope to reach them."

Personal Attributes of a Good Teacher

- Shows emotional maturity through self-control, sense of humor, sincerity, and objectivity
- Shows awareness of appearance by being neat, clean, and appropriately dressed
- Has enduring patience and kindness
- Is willing to accept responsibility for his or her actions
- Is always willing to try new techniques
- Is tactful
- Does critical thinking and evaluation
- Shows enthusiasm
- Is not discouraged by defeats or failures, but sees each day as a new chance
- Likes children
- Passes along compliments
- Has ability to make adjustments to fit any occasion
- Is an excellent organizer of time and materials to achieve the most effective results
- Has discipline that provides for effective teaching and results in good citizenship
- Instils intellectual curiosity and the desire for learning
- Has wide knowledge of subject matter
- Provides for individual differences

- Keeps accurate and up-to-date records
- Makes use of community resources
- Makes an effort to know parents
- Knows what is going on in the community and exercises the voting franchise with intelligence
- Has a sense of loyalty to parent, school, community, and country

Importance of Mental Health

All teachers must be emotionally well balanced. Bad temper and impatience are quickly sensed by students and can destroy the delicate student-teacher relationship. Of course, there are worries and anxieties that affect all of us, and teachers have their share. Yet an emotionally healthy teacher will take the daily frustrations for what they are. A good teacher will not magnify their importance.

It certainly is unfair for teachers to unburden themselves in the classroom. The fear and terror created by the moody, prejudiced, overly strict, or otherwise emotionally unstable teacher endangers the health of the pupils, just as a teacher suffering from tuberculosis endangers their physical health. School principals and superintendents are working hard to devise procedures for screening unstable personalities from teacher candidates.

In Angelo Patri's words, the well-adjusted teacher is one who:

> Can laugh, easily and often. There is no tension anywhere in his body, he swings along easily, with a light step, a shining happy look in his eyes. He takes the mistakes, the annoyances that are daily occurrences in the life of any teacher, with a smile and a shrug and says, "Well, well, tomorrow is another day. We'll begin again tomorrow."
> The healthy-minded teacher never bears a grudge. When there is something going wrong he goes directly to the source and says,

"How come? What's to do here? Tell me about it," and if necessary speaks clearly, even sharply, what is in his mind, a free clear
mind. Once having done so the matter is settled as far as he is concerned. He does not brood over wrong, either real or fancied. Nor
does the healthy-minded teacher lose self-control in times of stress.

A sign of the times is the increasing complaint teachers are voic-
ing about stress factors in the classroom. Administrators are already
helping teachers suffering from teaching "burnout" by giving them
leaves of absence, assigning them nonteaching jobs, or sending them
for psychotherapy.

A Columbia University Teachers College psychologist found that
unresponsive, uncooperative administrators were the most highly
perceived source of stress among approximately four hundred teachers surveyed in New York City. Other stress factors included lack
of cooperation from parents, a poor sense of community in the
schools, and nonrewarding contacts with colleagues.

If the human service professions, such as teaching, health care,
and social work, seem more prone to burnout, the survey's com-
pilers speculate that idealistic young people who chose such careers
during the 1960s expected more from their work than did their
contemporaries in more lucrative fields. Social conditions changed,
however, and instead of a sense of personal satisfaction, teachers
found themselves the targets of widespread and often virulent public criticism.

A study of college faculty from 1983 to 1986 by Jack H. Schus-
ter and Howard R. Bowen, coauthors of *American Professors: A Natural Resource Imperiled*, identified poor working conditions as one
cause of depression having a negative effect on morale. Many programs have been established by teacher federations with networks
for teachers to conduct awareness-building exercises and emotional
support systems. As one teacher-chairperson of a conference on

teacher stress explained, "Teachers give, give, and give all day. We want a program which will help teachers learn ways to renew themselves in their demanding jobs."

"For our faculty, the spirit of renewal is teacher talk," writes Suzanne Soo Hoo, principal of Carver Elementary School in Cerritos, California. "We hold meetings while students attend assemblies, and we convene staff retreats a couple of times a year. This 'quality time' is used to gain perspective and direction in our work."

What else can a teacher or any person in a stressful job do to relieve this stress? Professor Barry Farber, a psychologist at Columbia University Teachers College, suggests some measures:

- Acknowledge the problem.
- Try to change teaching assignments. Don't just teach fourth grade for thirty years.
- Press for more flexible work schedules so that all days do not seem alike.
- Ask the administration for stress-reduction workshops for long-term expression and outlet of teacher needs, concerns, and interests.
- Find an outside interest—jogging, theater, a hobby—that will provide the emotional payoff missing at work.

Realizing their own problems and those factors contributing to them helps teachers develop the characters of superior teachers.

Aware of the high pressures on the teacher, Bel Kaufman, a teacher who wrote the book *Up the Down Staircase*, addressed a New York United Federation of Teachers conference with these words of encouragement:

> You are the survivors, the non-dropouts. You have survived the pressures that go with your territory. You wield power you may

not be aware of, because you have the power to change the future for the children in your classroom. Each time you step into the classroom, there is the potential for greatness.

Reasons to Become a Teacher

The Department of Education released a booklet, *America's Children Are Counting on You: 10 Reasons to Become a Teacher.* They include:

1. To ignite the spark of curiosity in children.
2. To practice three of life's most valuable virtues: kindness, patience, and understanding.
3. To experience the joy of seeing children learn to read, write, and do arithmetic—and set them on a path to success in school and in life.
4. To share your love of learning with young minds and help students discover their potential.
5. To see the world through a child's eyes while sharing your knowledge—and to learn something in return.
6. To make the same kind of difference in a child's life as your favorite teacher made in yours.
7. To help children understand the diversity of cultures and values that make our country strong and proud.
8. To serve children, your community, and your country.
9. To turn your love of learning into a love of teaching.
10. To share your passion. If you like seeing a child's eyes light up with understanding, you belong in the classroom.

2

QUALIFICATIONS
AND TRAINING

IF YOU ARE seriously considering entering teaching as a career, it would be advisable for you to consult a guidance counselor or advisor to discuss your situation as fully as possible. Most high schools have excellent guidance facilities. Read as much of the available literature on teaching as possible. You will thus get a complete picture of the teaching field and learn whether you have the personal qualities necessary for success in this profession.

You might test your interest in teaching and your fondness of working with children further by taking a summer job in a camp, day school, neighborhood settlement, or community center. You might also join local teacher organizations such as the Future Teachers of America (FTA) to learn about teaching. These experiences can help you determine what age groups are best for you to work with.

Choosing a Teaching Level

Once you have decided on teaching as a career, you will have to make up your mind whether you want to teach in elementary school, high school, or college. Should you choose high school or college teaching, you will also have to decide on your major and minor fields of specialization. Teaching certificates are granted for specific kinds of teaching upon the completion of a prescribed course. Teachers must now take a teacher-certification exam in most states before they can receive certification.

Your college program will depend upon the specific phase of teaching in which you are interested. Be careful about this. You will save yourself a lot of wasted effort and frustration if you know beforehand the certification requirements of the state in which you want to teach, the age group you want to work with, the subject you want to teach, and the demand for teachers in each area of the field. Your decision to go into college teaching need not be made before entering college. In fact, it is usually experience with advanced study in college that draws young men and women into college teaching.

The Basics of Teacher Education

What courses should you take in high school if you wish to become a teacher? Usually the courses of a general or college preparatory program in high school are acceptable for admission to college. You will have to obtain a college degree regardless of your choice of teaching field. However, since admission requirements in colleges vary, ask your counselor or principal for help in planning your high school program. If you are permitted to take electives, take courses in the subjects that interest you. With the help of your school or local librarian, draw up a reading list to broaden your interests. Once you begin training, try to focus on one or two curriculum areas in which you plan to master your teaching craft. If, however, you have already selected the college or colleges that you would like to attend, write for their catalogs to learn about entrance requirements.

Several free publications are available from the U.S. Department of Education, including *Promising Practices: New Ways to Improve Teacher Quality* and *Meeting the Highly Qualified Teachers Challenge,* which contains examples of attempts to recruit talented and diverse people into the teaching profession and discusses licensing and certification standards.

How can you be sure whether you are eligible to get into a teacher education program? You will need a good high school academic record to meet the requirements of the college to which you are applying. Check with your guidance counselor about the requirements of the college of your choice.

Besides a good academic record, colleges are concerned with a student's health, personality, poise, and character. They may also consider your proficiency in English, your ability to communicate, and your outside activities and work experience. You might take a comprehensive inventory and try to correct any personal weaknesses as a first step in preparing for college admission.

What courses will you take once you get to college? There are more than fifteen hundred accredited colleges and universities in the United States that offer teacher education programs. Few of these programs are exactly alike. However, all have programs that will train you to be a teacher. Usually the first two years of your college career will be in liberal arts. The first two years will also help develop your personality and help you become a contributing member of your community.

When taking courses geared toward future teacher placement, you will have to bring the academic and professional education departments together. A first-grade teacher must be well versed in all the basic skills—history, mathematics, English, and other subjects. College teachers must keep up with all current research in their subjects.

In *A Time for Teaching*, Willard Abraham recommends that all teaching students study "to create a new alignment of liberal arts, specialized subject matter, and professional education." Since all areas are developing at a quick rate, the basic foundations of liberal arts must be supported by knowledge of specific subjects. Besides the academic areas, the author also identifies important ingredients of teacher education. He lists the following:

- Introduction to the physical and biological sciences
- Understanding of democracy—its meaning and background
- Knowledge of the historical, cultural, and sociological heritage of the United States
- Understanding of the world today
- Ability to read critically
- Knowledge of teaching methods
- Familiarity with psychology
- Ability to communicate

Preschool Teachers

Preschool teachers are teaching children who can range from just a few months to age five, as mothers are joining the workforce earlier than before. Private preschools are flourishing as new scientifically based research has shown that children can develop their language abilities and increase their knowledge during this young period. The Early Childhood–Head Start Task Force booklet

Teaching Our Youngest: A Guide for Preschool Teachers and Child Care and Family Providers offers suggestions for those who want to become preschool teachers. Some suggestions include reading aloud to children to increase their reading ability, providing a special classroom for children, and utilizing scientifically based reading research to obtain new methods for knowledge building.

Elementary Teaching Courses

If you plan to be an elementary teacher, about one-fourth of your college education will be devoted to courses in education. These elementary education courses include the study of the growth and development of children, methods of teaching, and child psychology. You will take courses in how to teach reading or, more specifically, how to teach reading to first-grade children. You will take courses in the psychology of learning and in practice teaching. Here you will actually be sent into a classroom where you will teach with the regular teacher.

You will also take courses in lesson planning. You will be taught how to prepare a lesson and how to motivate a class. You will follow a curriculum that will specifically train you for classroom teaching.

Secondary School Teaching Courses

If you plan to be a secondary school teacher, you will spend about one-seventh of your time in courses dealing with educational and adolescent psychology, tests and measurements, methods of teaching, and student teaching. About one-third of your college program will be devoted to the subject that you plan to teach. You must recognize that because secondary school subjects are more advanced, the teacher needs to have more preparation in the subject he or she teaches than does the elementary school teacher. In addition to your regular education program, you will have from three to six months of student teaching. Here you will actually go into the classroom and work with students.

An experienced master teacher will supervise you. Student teaching is conducted at campus laboratory schools, public schools, and, sometimes, private schools. In some cases you will live in the community where you do your student teaching. There you will meet the residents and become part of the community.

Becoming a College Teacher

If you plan to be a college teacher, your major preparation will be in your special subject. The college teacher is not usually required to have courses in the field of education unless he or she expects to teach education courses. However, you will be expected to complete postgraduate courses. Most college teachers are required to have a doctoral degree. A doctorate is your certificate of advanced study and proficiency in your field.

To obtain an assistant or associate professorship, extensive graduate training and college teaching experience is necessary. A full professor usually has ten to fifteen years of experience and has made some outstanding contribution in his or her specialty. Even for an instructor's position you will often need a doctorate. Sometimes graduate students are asked to assist in teaching undergraduates while they are completing their advanced work, offering them opportunities to gain teaching experience.

Schooling Alternatives

The National Center for Information on Careers in Education offers five alternatives for preparing for a school career in its booklet *Careers in Education*:

1. Enroll in a large university with an undergraduate school of education. Universities offer the opportunity to take liberal arts courses along with the required education courses. Such a program allows the student to enroll in a variety of courses.

2. Enroll in the traditionally accepted state teacher training institutions. Many of these schools successfully combine liberal arts with education courses and also offer on-site training.

3. Enroll in a community junior college. These schools can provide two years of preparation toward a bachelor's degree in the student's area of interest. This two-year program also allows the student to fulfill the requirements of basic courses needed for any area of specialization. The community setting often permits the student to participate in volunteer activities or to work as an aide in the field in which he or she hopes to specialize.

4. Enroll in a liberal arts college and receive a bachelor's degree in a specific area. After receiving the undergraduate degree, enroll in a graduate program that offers a master of arts in teaching degree (M.A.T.). Most M.A.T. programs, as well as others patterned after them, require time actually working in a classroom and getting supervised, on-the-job training.

5. Enroll as an education major in a cooperative program where the student studies on the campus part of the year and works at a remunerative job the other part of the year. Many institutions offer work-study programs within the school system.

The M.A.T. degree and other programs sponsored by colleges and universities make it possible for persons whose education has been in other fields to begin careers in education. In certain cases, such persons can gain classroom experience while they finish the requirements for certification. Special certification programs are available in some states for specialized groups such as military personnel and Peace Corps veterans.

Does the teachers college or education department you are looking into provide a sound liberal arts background? Is it alert to current developments in various fields? Can you pursue your interests? What practical facilities does it have for working with children? How much practice teaching does it offer? How strong is its faculty? How good is the library?

Writing for catalogs and information can be very helpful in answering these and other questions. If it is possible try to visit several colleges. Speak with the students. Attend a few classes. Set up personal interviews. The attitudes of both students and faculty members will tell you more about a school than will all the letter writing in the world. Many colleges have a pre-freshman day to help prospective students get acquainted with the school.

Other Alternate Routes

New ways to meet teacher shortages has transformed the teacher preparation process to what the Department of Education refers to as Alternative Routes to Teaching. Started in 2001, the Department of Education began developing alternate certification to the teaching profession by offering initial Passport Certification to teaching candidates with a bachelor's degree and mastery of the subject. An advanced Master Teacher credential was given beginning in 2004 to teachers with proficiency in their subjects and documented student gains.

Almost all 575 teacher preparation institutions accredited by the National Council for Accreditation of Teacher Education (NCATE) have postbaccalaureate programs that provide preparation for individuals who want to enter teaching but did not enroll in an education program while an undergraduate. There is a list of NCATE-accredited institutions on the Web with links directly to those institutions/colleges of education websites. More than 130 of these institutions have alternate route programs that reduce financial barriers to entry and are geared to adults looking for programs where they can draw a salary and/or receive a stipend during the period of career change. The NCATE's booklet *Answering the Call to Teach* provides useful information, including financial aid and distance-education information.

An alternative teaching route system has been formulated by the American Board for Certification of Teacher Excellence (ABCTE) that allows those passing the American Board assessment to be considered fully certified to teach, regardless of their education qualifications. This has not gained favor with the National Education Association (NEA) and other associations that do not approve of the testing-only approach to teacher licensure with NEA executive John Wilson commenting, "The message is that you don't need any formal preparation to become a teacher . . . everything you need to know can be gauged by a computer-based test." On the other side, ABCTE president Kathleen Madigan said, "We base certification not on whether an applicant has come up through the traditional route, such as a college of education, but on whether that teacher knows his or her academic content and classroom management skills."

Online Teacher Preparation Programs

Technology has now made possible online teacher-preparation programs as a form of competency-based distance-learning programs for teaching candidates. The Department of Education gave a five-year Star Schools grant beginning in 2001 to Western Governors University (WGU), an online consortium of nineteen western states and forty-five universities to develop an online K–8 licensure program. The Teachers College also offers associate degrees for para-professionals, designed for nontraditional candidates changing careers to become teachers and teachers who want to advance their education. Students are assigned a faculty mentor who designs their individual program and assesses candidates seeking initial certification; students also receive at least six months of supervised training in a K–12 school.

An online bachelor's degree with licensure in secondary-school mathematics or science, a postbaccalaureate licensing program in math and science for uncertified teachers and midcareer professionals, and master's degrees in teaching math or science are also offered.

This represents a new way for those in remote areas like Alaska or soldiers stationed in a foreign country and nearing retirement to log on to WGU to take necessary courses to become a teacher. More information can be obtained at wgu.edu/wgu/index.html. Some states are exploring this online model for teacher training; for example, the University of Maryland was awarded a $2 million Department of Education grant to develop its own online teacher certification program.

Selecting a College or University

Before you choose a college or university, it may be helpful to acquaint yourself with the certification requirements and the accredited training colleges in the state where you wish to teach.

You will find that almost every state has one or more publicly supported teachers colleges. Since these colleges prepare teachers for the public schools of a particular state, many require their students to sign a pledge to teach in that state for at least a year following graduation. A few states charge only nonresidents. Others that charge even the residents of the states make the tuition higher for nonresidents.

Guidance counselors can help students decide which college to choose. In 2002, according to *Education Statistics Quarterly 2003*, 77 percent of public schools indicated that selection of a career major or path was available and 50 percent of all public high schools required all students to participate in the activity of individual counseling sessions.

Besides the state teacher-training schools, there are private schools that train teachers. There are also courses of training provided by liberal arts colleges. Indeed, fifteen hundred institutions of higher learning offer courses that lead to a teaching certificate. In choosing your school, weigh carefully all the advantages offered by each type of institution. A good training course should combine a substantial background in methods and a well-rounded education in general studies.

Some teacher institutes, like the one at Yale University, have a joint program with the public school system. The program established in 1978 by the Yale Teachers Institute and the New Haven Public School system has been cited as a "promising model of university and school collaboration," where teachers, as fellows of the institute, work with Yale faculty members to develop innovative programs and receive supervision in their teaching.

Financing Your Education

As costs of all schools escalate, the prospective teacher can anticipate rising tuition costs. Fortunately, new federal grants and loan programs are being instituted to offset these high costs. Especially prevalent are work-study programs that give students valuable experience and help pay for school costs.

According to *The Condition of Education 2004*, by the National Center for Education Statistics, between 1990 and 2000 the average price of attending college (tuition and fees plus an allowance for living expenses) increased at public two-year institutions from $7,300 to $8,500, at public four-year institutions from $10,000 to $12,400, and at private four-year institutions from $19,400 to $24,400. Reflecting the higher cost, 71 percent of students received aid in 2000; 54 percent received aid in 1990.

The National Service Program, for example, gives college students the chance to repay their loans by participating in community service such as the Professional Service Corps in Teaching for one to two years.

Sources for financial assistance can be found at college admission offices and in their catalogs, in addition to government and privately funded aid programs.

Some financial assistance guides include the U.S. Department of Education's *The Student Guide*, available free from The Federal Student Aid Information Center, P.O. Box 84, Washington D.C., 20044, or you can find it on the Internet at ed.gov.

Scholarships, fellowships, loans, precollegiate recruitment programs, and other sources of financial assistance are increasing to help students finance their education despite rising tuition costs.

Licensing and Accreditation in Teacher Education

Teaching has become a very complex and responsible profession. Elementary and secondary school practitioners are licensed after they complete four years of courses at the college level. There is, indeed, a significant trend toward the requirement of a master's degree for teaching in secondary schools. Professional improvement is constantly emphasized on all levels, for teaching stands at the helm of human progress and must reflect the needs of a given time.

In the past, some of the finest teachers may not have even completed the ninth grade. One man recounts, "I remember a Sioux woman who teaches Sioux language and culture at the university who probably managed to finish the ninth grade. She could not teach at the high school because she lacked the certification to teach in that setting. Yet she has more to contribute than anyone else."

Before the creation of public school systems in the United States, teachers were, in effect, licensed by being hired. The first state certification system was instituted in Ohio in 1825; this system empowered county officials to examine candidates and issue certificates. Later, New York and Vermont placed this responsibility on county superintendents of schools. Generally, procedures of certification under these and later systems used standardized examinations or preparation requirements.

A system that originally placed responsibility for licensing of teachers in some three thousand local licensing authorities has been reduced to the fifty state systems and a handful of large city school districts, such as those of New York City and Chicago, which retain special authority.

According to the Commission on Undergraduate Education and Education of Teachers, the present requirements for teacher certification (elementary or secondary) can be divided into three categories:

1. Typically the states have citizenship, health, age, and moral requirements.
2. All states require a minimum of a bachelor's degree for certification.
3. A few states also require specialized courses in state history, state and federal government, agriculture, and conservation.

Several of these states accept passing scores on proficiency exams in lieu of courses.

An estimated forty-four states have enacted legislation to raise standards of eligibility for teacher education. The intended purpose is to eliminate candidates who do not possess the inherent skills to become a teacher. A total of thirty-five states in 2002 had developed and linked teacher certification requirements to student content standards.

Each state requires a different procedure in licensing the teacher. Some states use their own state exams, and many use both the exam and the National Teacher Examinations (NTE) Core Battery, the most popular teacher testing instrument. With the NTE Core Battery, each state sets its own passing grade. A statewide system for assessing beginning teachers' performances is also used in many states. According to the Department of Education's *Meeting the Highly Qualified Teachers Challenge* report, approximately 6 percent of the teaching force lacked full certification in 2001–02 and seven states reported more than 10 percent of teachers on waivers (teaching with emergency, temporary, or provisional licenses), especially in high-poverty school districts.

Licenses Necessary

Before you can teach in the public schools of any state, you have to meet certain standards set up by the particular state's department of education. Each state has its own requirements. The trend now is to make it easy for teachers to move to new positions in different states. According to the Department of Education's reports, a teacher who has good preparation from an accredited teacher-training institution can usually obtain regular certification in nearby states and in states where there is need for services, if the teacher promises to qualify for regular certification within a specified period of time. Some states now have certification requirements for teaching in publicly controlled colleges and universities.

A college degree from an accredited institution is almost always required for regular certification. Here is advice from the U.S. Department of Education: "Don't let certification worry you too much. Just make certain that the college you select meets the general regulations of the state department of education of the state in which you wish to teach, and be sure to see the college official responsible for coordinating the education program with state certification requirements."

You will find that requirements for certification to teach in the public schools vary from state to state. The requirements also vary according to the kind of teaching you are planning to do. New requirements are constantly being implemented. In general, remember that college teaching requires the greatest amount of educational preparation.

Elementary School

All states and the District of Columbia require public elementary school teachers to be certified by the department of education in the state in which they work. Some states also require certification of teachers in private and parochial schools. Four years of college education are required by all states; some states require teachers to have postgraduate education—usually a master's degree or a fifth year of study—within a certain period after their initial certification.

Most states have a minimum teaching age of eighteen years. Before you start on a teaching career, you should become acquainted with the specific requirements of the state in which you hope to teach.

High Schools

Although the requirements for a certificate on the high school level vary, the typical state will permit you to teach if you have a bachelor's degree and have taken a certain number of education courses. The state will expect you to have some practice teaching. You are expected to specialize in one or more courses that are found on the high school level. Several states will not grant you a teaching certificate unless you have taken at least one year of graduate work beyond the bachelor's degree.

As on the elementary level, many local communities have added further requirements, particularly in larger cities where more educational preparation, education courses, or practice teaching may be required. Nearly all states require that applicants pass a test of basic skills before they can be certified as teachers, and many states also require teachers to enroll in continuing education courses to renew their certificates.

It is important that you have sufficient courses and enough practice teaching to meet the minimum legal requirements of the state or the community in which you want to teach. For example, if you want to teach English, you should probably take a traditional liberal arts course of study for the first two years and then concentrate during the last two years on courses in English literature, grammar, Shakespeare, and other topics that are related to English. To make yourself an even more attractive job applicant, take courses in history or philosophy.

Many high schools, especially the smaller ones, ask their teachers to teach more than one subject. Indeed, even the larger school systems have found it necessary to transfer their teachers from English, where they have had an abundance of teachers, to a course in biology or science, where there have been fewer teachers. If you have a mastery of more than one subject, you will find job hunting that much easier.

While in college, you might also try to participate in extracurricular activities such as dramatics, debating, track, or student government. These activities will be to your credit when the principal or superintendent looks over your credentials and compares you to another candidate for the same position.

For complete information on certification requirements, consult *A Manual on Certification Requirements for School Personnel in the United States*, which can be obtained from the Superintendent of Documents, U.S. Government Printing Office, Washington, D.C. 20402.

Another compilation of state certification requirements can be found in *Requirements for Certification of Teachers, Counselors, Librarians, and Administrators for Elementary Schools, Secondary Schools, and Junior Colleges*. This book is written by Robert C. Woellner and M. Aurilla Wood and is revised annually. It is published by the University of Chicago Press.

For any other specific information about elementary, high school, or college teaching, you might write to either the U.S. Department of Education or the National Commission on Teacher Education and Professional Standards.

Junior Colleges

Some states have minimum requirements for two-year college teachers. To learn the requirements, you might write to selected state directors of two-year college education.

Three out of four community and junior college teachers have master's degrees, and many have doctorates. Special programs for community college teachers are offered in many four-year colleges and universities. These institutions enroll more than ten thousand students in courses related to teaching in two-year colleges. Sometimes experience in a particular subject may count for as much as formal education training.

Colleges

To get an initial appointment teaching at a college, instructors generally must have a master's degree. For advancement to higher ranks, they need further academic training as well as experience. Assistant professors usually need a year of graduate study beyond the master's degree and at least a year or two of experience as an instructor. Appointments as associate professors frequently demand a doctoral degree and an additional three years or more of college teaching experience. For full professorship, a doctorate and extensive teaching experience are essential.

Accreditation of Educational Programs

Many factors complicate accreditation of teacher preparation. Educators have cited pressure put on institutions from outside agencies as well as from the university itself, dependence of teacher education upon the total institutional program, different philosophies regarding the best method to prepare teachers, and the great diversity of specialization within teacher education. Two organizations accredit teacher education on the national level. The National Council for the Accreditation of Teacher Education (NCATE) and the National Association of State Directors of Teacher Education and Certification (NASDTEC) have developed standardized programs whose graduates reciprocally receive approval from other programs.

NCATE is the professional accrediting organization for schools, colleges, and departments of education in the United States. It is a coalition of more than thirty organizations representing teachers, teacher educators, policymakers, and the public. NCATE's *Guide to College Programs in Teacher Preparation* can help you get through the process of accreditation. For information contact NCATE, 2010 Massachusetts Avenue NW, Suite 500, Washington, D.C. 20036-1023. Its website is ncate.org.

The NASDTEC standards contain listings of important groups and state agencies that grant reciprocity. They cite the NCATE and the six regional accrediting agencies: Middle States Association of Colleges and Secondary Schools, New England Association of Colleges and Secondary Schools, North Central Association of Colleges and Secondary Schools, Northwest Association of Secondary and Higher Schools, Southern Association of Colleges and Schools, and Western Association of Schools and Colleges. Each of these bodies has certain unique functions, but their purposes and procedures are similar.

The U.S. Department of Education maintains lists of accrediting agencies and state agencies that have been recognized by the secretary of education as reliable authorities concerning the quality of education presented at a particular school.

The Accreditation and Institutional Eligibility Staff evaluates accrediting agencies every four years to ensure they are continuing to meet the criteria set for accrediting agencies.

A revised copy of its publication, *Criteria for Nationally Recognized Accrediting Agencies and Associations*, can be obtained from the Accreditation and Institutional Eligibility Staff, U.S. Department of Education, 400 Maryland Avenue SW, Washington, D.C. 20202.

The National Education Association (NEA) gives other information about governance of the teaching profession from its Office for Instruction and Professional Development, 1201 Sixteenth Street NW, Washington, D.C. 20036.

Teacher Testing

Teachers, like lawyers, doctors, and other professionals, must take certification exams that test their basic abilities. Organizations like the Carnegie Forum on Education are recommending a different method of testing, such as a national certification board for teachers, which would simulate classroom situations. Teachers often balk at the tests, which, they claim, cannot truly test their ability or their knowledge. The issue of teacher competency will be increasing as students' abilities reflect their teachers' skills.

The teacher education and certification reforms that were suggested in the late 1980s and early 1990s are said to affect qualifications of the teacher workforce in the year 2005. The Carnegie Forum on Education and the Economy and the Holmes Group have proposed that all teachers receive a comprehensive liberal arts education at the undergraduate level.

On Reforming Teacher Education

Noted English biologist Thomas Henry Huxley once said, "Perhaps the most valuable result of all education is the ability to make yourself do the thing you have to do, when it ought to be done, whether you like it or not. This is perhaps the first lesson to be learned." Unfortunately, many teachers regard education not as preparation for life but as a way to earn a living. The Study Commission on Teacher Education interviewed many students and determined that future teachers needed to broaden their education to better relate to the community and services around them. The report states, "If teachers-to-be are to regard education as an enterprise which extends beyond the school door, their own intellectual, vocational, and social life at the college or institution of higher education ought to form a single continuum so that this intellectual life does not stop when they go to their living unit."

"Teacher education must help prepare those teachers for the jobs available to them," declares Donald McCarty in his book *New Perspectives on Teacher Education*. He goes on to say, "One cannot plan for the training of educators . . . without prior consideration of children, the culture, and the schools."

According to some educators, teacher preparation programs should not only prepare students to teach school but provide them with the necessary skills to enter other vocations in every area. Thus teacher education is recommended to prepare trainees for a wide range of human services vocations.

Teacher education reform is often related to school reform. Teachers must be involved in planning, carrying out, and evaluating reform in education and in teacher education, some educators insist. They say that public instruction and teacher education must be closely related. Parents and students are also urged to be involved in the reform of education.

What many educators call the "careerism" of the 1970s and 1980s has a definite impact on the present school system. Teachers can no longer hide behind books, hoping the student will be able to make valuable use of the knowledge. The National Advisory Council of Education Professions Development had first advocated reform in teacher education training in its 1976 findings, suggesting that "an emphasis on the real world of schools and their specific needs and objectives are needed improvements in the process of educating teachers, which applies now more than ever."

Raising Standards

Education Boards are scrutinizing teachers like never before. Authors and parents have started correlating student scores with the teachers' own preparation and training.

New legislation like the No Child Left Behind Act requires that all teachers in core academic areas be "highly qualified" not later than the end of the 2005–06 school year. Core academic subjects are defined as English, reading or language arts, mathematics, science, foreign language, civics and government, economics, art, history, and geography.

Elementary school teachers who want to teach in New York will need thirty credits in the liberal arts, including some courses in a foreign language, math, science, and history, in addition to majoring in education. Teacher education programs will have to be accredited by a national accrediting body instead of a state organization, and teaching programs not meeting state standards would be closed down.

Another requirement that other states might impose is that all teachers be trained to teach children with disabilities, regardless of whether the teachers have degrees in special education. Conversely, those who plan to teach special education will need an undergraduate major in the arts and sciences. Teachers who earn a master's degree in education must take at least twelve additional credits in an academic subject area.

A law in Texas now requires that 70 percent of a training program's graduating teachers must pass the state exam or the program can lose accreditation.

Findings show that the scores of students improve on standardized tests in direct relation to the amount of training their teachers have in the subjects they teach, especially for math and science. In a measure to further increase a teacher's general skill and to maintain accreditation, teacher education programs also require classes in the use of computers and knowledge of other technologies.

From the emphasis on teacher competency testing in the 1980s came the concept of accountability in the 1990s to the concept of higher standards and lower barriers in the early 2000s. This naturally leads to an increased professionalization of the teacher workforce. There is more of an emphasis on subject matter competence in the No Child Left Behind Act than full teacher certification. New innovative methods of obtaining teaching certification have been recommended to adapt to the changing times. Since 1990, the number of teachers receiving alternative certification has doubled.

These programs are attracting those talented bachelor's degree holders who can begin teaching almost immediately. By getting instruction in teaching theory and classroom management during the summer before the school year, they become certified. This method adopts some of the characteristics of private businesses, focusing on outcome, accountability, the use of incentives linked to school performance, and devolution of authority.

Some of these programs include Troops to Teachers, where former members of the military join the teaching profession with ABCTE Board certification, and California's Technology to Teachers program, where laid-off technology workers are given the opportunity to enter the classroom. NOVA and the Silicon Valley Workforce Investment Network (SWIN) run the Technology to Teachers program in Santa Clara County, California, and work with universities and the South Bay Teacher Recruitment Center. Candidates must hold a bachelor's degree, pass the CBEST (the state's basic-skills test for teachers), and demonstrate competency in their field of teaching. Candidates can enter the classroom immediately or take courses necessary for certification. Anthony Silk, a laid-off high-tech employee who became a math teacher at Cupertino High in Silicon Valley, had this to say about the program: "My new career as teacher is much more rewarding than high-tech." More information on the SWIN Technology to Teachers program can be found at tech2teacher.org.

In-Service Training

The increase in the number of students who go on to higher education means an increase in the number of university graduates who want to go into teaching. But schools of education are beginning to realize that as teachers take on new roles, schools must also address the problems and needs of practicing school teachers. Many educators believe that teachers should continue to receive training and retraining throughout their careers. A Japanese report states that the "attempt to integrate the whole process of teacher training and retraining is inseparable related to the recent concept of the teaching profession." Teachers' unions are also recognizing not only the need but also the right of teachers to in-service training. As such training becomes more common, teachers as well as other educators are developing programs to meet training needs. Teacher centers outside schools of education have also developed to assist in this in-service training.

Minority Education

One of the most common criticisms of teacher education is that there is not enough exposure to learning about teaching minority groups. Rules, language, behavior, and cognitive systems oriented toward Anglo-Saxon, middle-class values are not effective in a minority setting and are likely to result in resentment and alienation among the students. Although a standardized concept of education may work for some children whose world is highly oriented to middle-class codes, for millions of other children it does not.

The Study Commission on Undergraduate Education and the Education of Teachers said that fewer than 3 percent of the non-English-speaking students who need bilingual-bicultural teachers have them. Many rural and Indian reservation areas, for example, continue to suffer real shortages of competent teachers. Teaching minority groups and recruiting minority groups to teach is being increasingly explored.

Special Education

Special education as foreseen in 2004 and beyond is embracing ways to better educate the child with special needs, and teachers will play an important and vital role. "Inclusion" is the latest in a series of evolving strategies for special-needs education used by educators, helping a child with a disability become a full part of the class. Instead of "mainstreaming" the special child inside classrooms and expecting them to keep up, inclusion involves rearranging the class—both the physical space and the curriculum—to include the child so that impaired and nonimpaired children can come to see one another as peers and learn while educating each other.

Teachers must learn new skills in special education within the classroom. The New York City school system created more than one thousand classes in 2003 that have met the definition of inclusion. "This is a step beyond for us," said Linda Wernikoff, New York City deputy superintendent for special-education initiatives, who helped create the program.

Bilingual Education

As more and more non-English-speaking students will be entering the system, teachers of bilingual education will increasingly be trained to identify students whose lack of language skills can be due to legal and social problems.

Among some of the goals that the National Council on Bilingual Education (NCBE) states in its manifesto are "equity and excellence for all students," "academic success and high standards for all students," "professional development initiatives for teachers," and "accelerated education programs for limited English proficient students."

NCBE offers its publications, which range from articles to guides, through its website ncbe.gwu.edu in collaboration with George Washington University. More college preparatory courses for minority students have been urgently recommended to improve the numbers of minority students becoming teachers, and future minority recruitment efforts should target teacher education programs to introduce greater ethnic diversity among teachers.

Other bilingual education organizations to contact for information about teaching opportunities include the National Association of Bilingual Education, a nonprofit organization "dedicated to promoting education excellence and equity for English language learners and representing the professional educators who serve them, such as teachers, administrators, college instructors, and other advocates for language-minority children." Go to nabe.org. The Office of English Language Acquisition, Language Enhancement, and Academic Achievement for Limited English Proficient Students (OELA) identifies major issues affecting the education of English language learners and assists state and local reform efforts. It promotes high-quality education for English language learners (ELLs) to a population known as limited English proficient students (LEPs).

3

How to Get Started

Once you have decided that teaching will be your life's work, you will have to think about getting a job. Even though at first you will be concentrating on your schooling, it's a good idea to find out as much as you can about the standards you will have to meet later on.

A good record of achievement, leadership qualities, and the ability to work with others go a long way when it comes to recommendations. Teachers take note of capable students. They know how important adaptability and other personal characteristics are in teaching. School boards, too, know what they want in a teacher to whom they entrust the children of their communities. They also know which schools usually prepare reliable teachers.

Understanding Yourself

Applying for a teaching position requires two basic steps. First, you must make a frank, searching self-appraisal of yourself to make sure you are qualified. You must study your strengths and weaknesses. This self-analysis can be aided by joining clubs and organizations and then assessing your community participation.

Information about yourself also helps you determine if teaching is the right career for you. Health examinations, speech tests, achievement tests, and other indicators will show if you can last in a teaching job.

Understanding Teaching

Getting a clear understanding of what teaching is must be the first step the teacher-to-be takes. The book *Teaching as a Career* gives three descriptions of teaching:

1. Teaching is a full-time occupation.
2. Teachers teach a full, organized body of knowledge.
3. What teachers teach is chosen for its value to pupils.

Preparation is essential for any applicant. Often it serves an applicant well to visit a school he or she once attended. If you visit a former school, you can observe some of the problems and rewards that teaching brings. Visit former teachers and perhaps even sit in some of the classrooms to see if the teachers are still as good or bad as you remembered. Often the desire to become a teacher stems from early school experience.

When applying for a job, keep several things in mind. You must question what community resources will be available to you. Is there a professional library in the town? How are the teachers assigned in the school? Will assignments be made to different grades and schools within the system? If you can answer some or all of these questions after you inquire about the school, you are prepared to consider accepting or rejecting a teaching job.

Jane Waldman is an elementary school teacher who reentered the teaching profession after a nearly five-year absence. She explains how she got her elementary teaching position at a Miami, Florida, school. "When I reentered the teaching profession, I first took administrative steps," said Jane. "I went to the Board of Education and got my papers. Then I went personally to schools, which I found better than sending letters.

"Gradually I saw that I could see people, and it was easier as time went on. I decided to substitute teach until the principal recommended me for a permanent substitute position until the teacher returned in six months. This left my options open if I wanted a permanent job." Jane got a permanent teaching job and said, "I've grown with the job. What was difficult and frustrating about teaching, I now find inspiring."

Job Placement

Except in certain large cities where a potential teacher must pass a competitive examination to become eligible for a job, you may register as a candidate for a position as soon as you complete your education. There are several avenues you should explore in looking for employment.

• You may use the college placement office. Most colleges maintain a placement bureau that keeps itself informed of school conditions and job openings. These bureaus draw vacancies to the attention of graduating students and are successful in placing a majority of teaching candidates. The procedure works in this fash-

ion: School superintendents send vacancy notices to college placement bureaus and ask them to recommend eligible students. It is
assumed that the college offices know their own students and that
they will consult with members of the teaching staff in selecting
the best candidates for the jobs.

• You may use commercial teachers' agencies. These agencies
perform services similar to the college placement offices for a fee.
In localities where there is an overabundance of candidates, it is
advantageous to register with a commercial agency. If you wish to
teach in a particular city, get in touch with an agency in that area.

• You may apply directly. In areas where there are few teachers
colleges and only a handful of candidates, applying directly to
school superintendents is an effective method of securing a job. In
overcrowded teaching areas, this method is not advisable. In fact,
it usually involves a lot of wasted time and effort for both the job
seeker and the school superintendent, who is bombarded with hun-
dreds of requests. Before making a direct application, talk it over
with your college placement office.

• Many schools consider their student teaching programs a
direct means of recruiting new teachers. Under this system, school
principals and superintendents have occasion to observe the student
teacher, and, at the same time, the student is given an opportunity
to experience the working situation in a particular school. He or
she can then use the experience as a basis for deciding whether he
or she would like to teach in that school.

Making Contact

The letter-writing process is similar in secondary and elementary
schools and colleges. In the public schools, the letter is addressed
to the superintendent. In private schools, the letter is written to the

principal. In colleges, the letter usually goes to the department head.

One method of obtaining a position is to submit, in writing, your qualifications for certification in the state departments of education of several adjoining states. Having obtained certification, you can then seek a post in the state or states in which you've been granted certification. Applying in several adjoining states makes it easier to appear for personal interviews. It would be unusual for a school administrator to employ a teacher on the basis of only a written application.

If you are inquiring about a job, it would be best to start the letter like this:

> Dear Mr. Thompson:
> I would like to apply for a position of teaching at Cardinal High School. I expect to receive my B.A. at the end of this year. Enclosed you will find my résumé.

If you are writing a letter of application after being referred by an agency or college placement office, the letter would differ:

> Dear Mrs. Chase:
> It was suggested that I get in touch with you about a teaching position opening at Beavercreek Elementary School this fall.

A letter replying to an advertisement in a newspaper or professional journal is direct:

> Dear Mrs. Hill:
> Enclosed you will find my résumé for the position of teaching advertised in the June 12 *Tribune*.

The letter should ask for an interview. Teachers are always interviewed personally, because demeanor and personality are so vital to a teacher's position.

After a successful interview, your follow-up letter might read as follows:

> Dear Mr. Brown,
>   I certainly enjoyed speaking with you last Tuesday about Rollins College and the position of mathematics professor. I look forward to hearing from you.

Later, write another follow-up letter if you have not heard anything from the potential employer:

> Dear Mr. Brown:
>   It has been two weeks since I came to Rollins College for an interview for the opening of mathematics professor. I hope you will let me know your decision.

The final letter is the one of acceptance:

> Dear Mr. Brown,
>   I am delighted to accept the position of mathematics professor at Rollins College for the fall term. I hope you will send me final details.

Assessing Your Options

Once you get past the first steps and get accepted to the inner circle of teacher-to-be applicants, you must realize there is keen competition for the most desirable jobs. Studies have shown that although enrollment is projected to be on the increase in the next decade and more teachers will be needed, there is still little turnover for the most popular teaching positions, such as physical and special education.

"Probably you don't see a rapid replacement of physical education teachers, because we stick around longer—we enjoy this job," says Ken Fine, a former physical education teacher of twenty years at Theodore Roosevelt High School in the Bronx, New York.

Because of this decreased demand, students entering the physical and health education programs at the upper division teacher education program at the University of Connecticut's School of Education are also prepared for a career in sports industries and recreational service education.

Reduction in teacher demand has also allowed schools of education to concentrate on long-neglected pedagogical research and development activities. Many institutions help prepare teachers to engage in research and development that will improve classroom performance and contribute to work with outside research agencies.

Many college placement offices continue to place beginning teachers successfully. But teaching students are being constantly made aware of new facets in their own education that will lead to broader dimensions in job placement.

Sometimes it is good to study two subjects, such as science and special education. "I have often had to teach science when I cannot teach my preference of special education," says science and special education teacher Anita Tavernier. "I think so many teachers like special education because it is very rewarding, and the classes are small. But I am glad that I can alternate with teaching science."

College Teaching

Job placements on the college level are often a matter of personal contact and recommendation. Customarily, all graduate students choose a professor under whom they do the major portion of their work. Through the sponsoring professors (as they are called), the student receives introductions to professors on the faculty at other colleges. When a college position is open, the department head consults with professors and asks them to refer promising doctoral candidates. Many institutions also employ postgraduate students as part-time instructors and later promote them to the full-time teaching staff.

One good way to get acquainted with college faculty types is to join professional organizations. Some organizations permit interested college students to participate in their activities on a limited basis. By meeting the other members of these organizations, you can get to know the people with whom you will be spending a good part of your life as a teacher and gain insight into the structure of the profession and its problems.

Colleges and universities do not usually employ teachers from direct applications. The responsibility for securing a new member of the staff is usually that of the chairperson of the department in which the vacancy exists. The department head may work in collaboration with a committee appointed by the dean or president of the institution.

This is the advice given by the U.S. Department of Education concerning securing a college teaching position:

> Applications for positions are usually solicited by letters to graduate schools or to the chairpersons of departments of the subject field in which the vacancy exists in other institutions. Institutions with strong graduate departments frequently select new staff among their own graduate students. In general, the employment of college teachers is highly personalized and depends very much upon personal recommendations between college officials who are well known to each other through professional relationships.

The American Association of Community and Junior Colleges recommends six steps in applying for a faculty position.

1. Determine whether there are vacancies in your particular field by calling the colleges or by writing to the state directors for community colleges.

2. Write to the appropriate department chairperson or dean outlining your interest and include a résumé.
3. Know the job requirements.
4. Describe your special qualifications.
5. Learn about the particular college.
6. Have background knowledge of the philosophy of the community and junior colleges.

How Teachers Are Selected

Naturally, boards of education and school administrators want to hire the most able teachers they can find. In determining which candidates are most suitable, they can use one of two techniques.

1. They can give competitive examinations. Several large cities, such as New York, Buffalo, and Newark, give examinations to applicants and draw up eligibility lists on which the names of candidates are placed in the order of their grades.

2. They can use personal interviews and evaluation of college records and experience. Most cities and towns utilize this more informal procedure for selecting teachers. A candidate's experiences, educational background, and letters of recommendation are carefully considered. In addition, he or she is interviewed by the school principal or superintendent and sometimes by both. Some schools request a teaching test in which the candidate takes over the activities of a class for a period of time.

By weighing the results of these procedures, the employer decides on the general fitness of each candidate and offers positions to the most qualified teachers.

There are innumerable reasons why beginners fail to receive teaching appointments. Unfortunately, the most common reason is ignorance of the required qualifications. After working hard in college and completing your credits, it is a shame to be rejected for a position just because you were negligent in making sure of the exact qualifications for the job you wanted.

Often beginners are too particular about the type of school or the location of the school they want to teach at. This is not realistic. Do not throw away appointments because the position does not measure up, point by point, to your image of the ideal job.

Remember that experience is the most desired qualification in an applicant. Once you have the experience, you can afford to pick and choose.

Other reasons for failing to secure a position include poorly written letters of application, unfavorable impressions in interviews, and lack of letters of recommendation from former teachers and training supervisors.

Although lack of personal or professional qualifications appropriate to the position desired is probably the most common cause for failure to secure employment, qualified teachers often fail to secure notification of vacancies and responses to their applications for positions. A self-addressed, stamped postcard enclosed with the application will usually ensure acknowledgment of your letter.

How the interviewer judges you is extremely important. Robert Krajewski, an associate professor of educational administration and supervision at a Texas state technical university, wrote in his article "I Never Met a Teacher I Didn't Like" that a principal respects his or her teachers. He says that every time he feels a "professional low" he brings two ideas to mind that help both the principal and teacher to function together and with the students.

First, Mr. Krajewski says, "Think positive." Problems diminish faster when practicing this policy. Second, he proposes the "KAR-R" method (know, accept, respect-respect). By developing knowledge of yourself, you can respect others. Teachers can gain the respect of their students and superiors by listening and accepting other people's ideas.

These are important points when seeking a job. Impressions last a long time. Basic foundations of good qualities build a person and a teacher into a leader.

You might have to create your own opportunities to show you are a leader. "I have to volunteer. I have to look for opportunities," said teacher Ann Brock from Texas. "If you wait until you are asked, you will not ever be asked, because people don't know that you are interested."

Paths to Advancement

After obtaining a teaching job, a person has constant opportunity to improve his or her professional standing. In both primary and secondary schools, child guidance programs are expanding, and schools look to their teachers to keep up with new methods. New kinds of educational specialties have made their appearance in the schools and have provided teachers with opportunities for advancement within the school system.

For those interested more in administrative work, each school has its principal and assistant principal. One of the top jobs in the field is that of the district superintendent, who is responsible for coordinating the schools within a certain area. Naturally, these jobs pay well and require experience and training beyond that of the classroom teacher.

Going from the high schools to the colleges, opportunities for advancement are equally plentiful. The structure of the college is held together by its deans and professors. At the head is the college president, one of the most highly prized and influential positions in the field of higher education.

Advancement in the School System

Here are some of the typical positions found in the average school system together with descriptions of the normal accepted paths for advancement.

School Teacher

The first step up the ladder is that of school teacher. Before you can become a specialist or an expert in school administration, you must start as a teacher. You can get your appointment, as has already been pointed out, by applying directly to the school superintendent, through the college placement bureau, or through a commercial placement agency. Occasionally there are exceptions to this rule.

Some state commissioners or county superintendents never were classroom teachers. But usually administrators are drawn from the ranks of the teaching profession.

Department Head

The next step up the academic ladder is that of department head. If, for example, you are a high school English teacher and are interested in administrative problems, you might strive to become the head of your school's English department.

In the large cities, such as New York, department heads have to take thorough examinations to test their intelligence, administrative ability, general knowledge, and academic competence. In other systems, the principal may have the right to appoint his or her own department heads. He or she will base the selection on the type of work performed by the teacher in the classroom.

Assistant Principal

The third step in the normal advancement of the school teacher is that of assistant principal. Here, too, brains and ability count more than influence. The teacher who does a good job, who is appointed head of the department, and who shows competence stands a good chance of becoming an assistant principal when a vacancy arises. This position is an excellent spot to show administrative ability. In some communities, the assistant principal is selected through a series of tests and interviews. In others, the superintendent or the board of education makes the appointment.

Director of School Division

Many of the larger school systems have divisional directors. For example, you may find in many schools a director of guidance, a director of personnel, a research director, a curriculum director, and directors of music, foreign languages, physical education, or, indeed, any one of a dozen or more departments.

School directors play an important part in the life of the educational system. They are assigned to many of the major problems in the school program. Often the higher posts in the system come from the ranks of directors who have been tried and have done well.

School Principal

The principal is usually selected by the superintendent of schools or, in the larger cities, through comprehensive examinations. Once you reach the post of school principal, you have earned a name for yourself. Both in prestige and in higher salary, a school principalship is a step forward. Of course, in the larger systems, the principal, whether on the elementary or high school level, is in an enviable position.

The principal meets the leading citizens of the community. A principal is frequently invited to address the parents or local civic groups. He or she is in a position to exert influence, for good or bad, on the school program. A poor principal can ruin the best school system.

Many of the smaller schools expect their principals to teach as well as to serve as administrative head. Sometimes, in rural schools, the principal is merely one of the teachers who has received an empty honor in being called the administrative head of the school. But, empty or not, it is an opportunity—one of the most important steps for improving your standing in the teaching profession.

Assistant or Associate Superintendent

This is an important administrative position that is attained only after a great deal of experience. The job is an important one and requires tact, forbearance, keen intelligence, and the ability to get along with colleagues and members of the community.

School Superintendent

The final rung in the ladder is the post of superintendent of schools. This is an appointed position to which men and women of competence and recognized ability should feel free to apply. But before the school board acts favorably upon an application, it wants answers to a host of questions. What is your educational background? How much actual experience did you have in the school system? What is your reputation for tact? Honesty? Integrity? Initiative? Imagination? Vision? Do you mingle well with other people? Do you have a pleasing personality? Has your past record been free of scandals or unpleasant controversies?

Seems foreboding, doesn't it? Actually, it is not as bad as it sounds. Frequently, school superintendents are chosen from within the school's own ranks—if a small city in Massachusetts is seeking a school superintendent, it may look to its own principals or directors for talent. Or the town may turn to other school systems and select a person who is already a school superintendent. By offering more money and a larger school, the town may induce the superintendent to leave his or her present post.

The school superintendent is the boss in deciding how the school system is to be run, who are to be employed as principals, what teachers are to be hired, and what policies are to be set up. He or she has considerable influence in the community.

Each state or each city sets up its own qualifications for the position of school superintendent. Normally a superintendent is required to hold a teacher's certificate, to have had five years or more of teaching experience, to have had experience as a principal or other top-ranking administrator, and to hold a master's degree or its equivalent.

Advancement at the College Level

At the college level, the paths of advancement are likewise fairly constant. First of all, you must have taken graduate work toward a master's or doctorate degree. There are instances, of course, of college instructors who have no degree beyond a bachelor's. If you want to advance in collegiate work, however, you will have to have either a master's or doctorate degree.

There has been an increased use of adjunct, or part-time, faculty. Here are a few steps you might normally expect for faculty advancement.

Graduate Assistant or Fellow

Many colleges or universities offer part-time assistantships or fellowships for their graduate students. While majoring in mathematics, for example, you may get the job of graduate assistant in the mathematics department. This appointment may entail anything from correcting papers to actually teaching one or more classes under the direction of your departmental head.

After you have proven yourself as a graduate assistant, you are in line for other academic posts. As long as you are working for your graduate degree, you will find yourself in a dual role—that of student and of teacher. This will give you an opportunity to decide whether you want to continue with teaching as a career or to branch off into research or further study.

Adjunct Professor

The adjunct professor's role has increased dramatically in the university and college. According to the Department of Education, adjunct professors accounted for two-thirds of all new professors hired in 2002–03 and the numbers keep increasing. Adjunct professors are untenured, and they work without benefits or job security. These limitations are serious, but taking a position as an adjunct professor is often the first step toward becoming a tenured faculty member. An average salary per course for adjunct professors in 2002–03 was $2,500 per course, and many teach at several colleges. The adjunct professors at Palomar College in San Maros, California, for example, receive $40.71 an hour, equaling to only $11,000 for the year, compared to the full-time professor's salary there of $69,170. Clearly many do not take the position for financial reasons.

Sandy Halland, an adjunct professor for the past ten years in the Boston area, commented in an interview, "There have been many times when I've said to myself, 'This is absolutely stupid, I've got to be out of my mind to do this.' I love to teach. And I think if you talk to any adjunct, that would be at the root of it. They simply love to teach."

Instructor

The first full-time position on the college faculty is that of instructor. It is usually offered to younger men and women just out of graduate school. The pay is not too high—the average salary in 2003 was $37,805, ranging from $34,165 to $44,716, and the work is fairly demanding. Here, too, you must prove yourself before you will be allowed to go forward along the path of advancement. If you have not as yet secured your doctorate degree, this would be the time to complete the academic requirements for it. You will find that once you enter the academic world on the collegiate level, degrees and academic honors mean a great deal if you want to advance. A lecturer is similar to an instructor but slightly more elevated, reflected by the median salary of $43,914 in 2003.

Assistant Professor

The next step, and the one that brings with it the greatest improvement in your status, is that of assistant professor. Once you move from the rank of instructor to assistant professor, you make a big jump. You might be responsible for one or more undergraduate courses, and you could be expected to publish scholarly articles or a book as well. The average salary for an assistant professor in 2002–03 was $51,545.

Associate Professor

After a certain length of time—usually anywhere from one to five years—the assistant professor is in line for advancement to associate professor. The rank of associate usually brings with it tenure—a guarantee of a permanent job. The promotion is made on the basis of demonstrated ability and through the recommendation of the head of the department or the university president. This position carries with it greater academic responsibilities and requires the publication of original research papers that are scholarly, authoritative, and contribute to the knowledge of the field. Duties can include supervising doctoral dissertations. The average salary for an associate professor in 2002–03 was $61,732.

Full Professor

The full professor is the highest academic rank you can achieve on the faculty (not including administrative posts). It is not easy, in many colleges, to jump from associate professor to professor. Some people never make it. Others have to wait years and years. The top colleges and universities consider the position of professor to be so important that it is reserved for those who have shown considerable academic standing, prestige, and competence.

In some colleges, the professors are the governing members of the faculty and make decisions concerning academic problems. The rate of pay is increased with promotion. It is a high honor to become a professor in an American institution of higher learning. In a 2002–03 survey by the American Association of University Professors, salaries for full professors in the United States averaged $86,437. Faculty in four-year institutions earn higher salaries, on average, than do those in two-year schools. In 2002–03, average faculty salaries in public institutions—$63,974—were lower than those in private independent institutions—$74,359—but higher than those in religiously affiliated private colleges and universities—$57,564.

In addition to academic positions, every college has a number of administrative jobs. These are usually appointed positions; that is, the president or the trustees have the power of appointing you, whether or not you are a member of the particular institution. Here are a few of these administrative positions.

Academic Dean

The dean is the head of a department, division, or school within a college or university. For example, Ohio State University has a dean of the school of education; Columbia University has a dean of engineering; New York University has a dean of the school of medicine. The dean frequently has had experience as a professor in that branch of academic activity, but that is not necessarily the case. He or she may be an outstanding individual with a reputation in the field of business, industry, government, or labor. The American Association of Teacher Education made a 2004 survey on deans and found that before becoming a dean, nearly 49 percent first served as department chairs, 25 percent were associate deans, and 18 percent had been department heads, proving that the proverbial step on the academic ladder can lead upward. A dean's salary can range from $107,414 as a dean of the business school to $41,050 as a dean of student activities.

Administrative Dean

As opposed to the academic dean, the administrative dean works closely with the administrative details of the institution. For example, most colleges and universities employ deans of men and women. They guide the college's activities along nonacademic lines. They maintain decorum, punish students for breaking rules, and in other ways keep order on the campus.

Registrar and Admissions Director

Anyone connected with colleges or universities knows that the admissions director and the college registrar have extremely important jobs. They are the first line of contact with the student body and with the public. The admissions director selects the students who are to enter the college. The director must be a person of ability, of exhaustive patience, and of extreme tact. You cannot knock on the college door and expect to become registrar or admissions director. Long administrative experience is required. Also, you must have worked on the college level in other administrative posts, such as assistant director or graduate fellow. If you hold a degree in the field of administration, it will help.

Assistant to the President

Many college presidents appoint assistants to aid them in their work. This position is a good stepping-stone to other high academic positions. As an assistant, you may be expected to know such fields as public relations, administration, and fund-raising. Also, you may be asked to substitute for the president when he or she is away.

Vice President

Most colleges have one or more vice presidents on their staff. For example, a university may have a vice president in charge of public relations and a vice president in charge of finances. Just as big business and industry may have a series of vice presidents, many colleges now follow the same pattern. However, there may be just one or two vice presidents. This is an important position and frequently leads to the top position of president.

College President

This post is the top position in a university, achieved only by persons of outstanding ability and experience—men and women of distinction from both the academic world and from other fields, such as the army, navy, government, and journalism. College presidents not only must be proven administrators of worth, but also outstanding educators with dynamic personalities who can bring to their job intelligence, expressiveness, and the combined abilities of the school teacher and the powerful businessperson.

Salaries for college presidents from 1997–98 (at a median salary of $100,000) to the 2002–03 school year have risen by approximately 33 percent, rivaling those of any powerful company CEOs. The overall compensation packages of presidents at four private universities exceeded $800,000, while presidents at twelve public universities earned more than $500,000 for the 2003–04 academic year.

The college president has the opportunity to lead the faculty to unified and individual achievements, to develop the local and national—perhaps international—standing of the school in one or more areas, and to create a dynamic focus for growth that will attract outstanding students and teachers to the college as a center of progress in study and research. Many great teachers who have become college presidents have influenced a generation or more of students in their institutions and made their work a lasting and memorable contribution to education.

"There was a time when a university president consulted with the faculty, consulted with the trustees, consulted with the student body president," said Gerhard Caspar, former president of Stanford University. "But now we are expected to consult with myriad caucuses, representing myriad views of the world."

The role of university president has assumed an important position. The president must lead the institution into higher academic realms and guide the college in dealing with various issues that can range from environmental concerns and sexual harassment to changing government regulations. The higher salaries and increased perks of college and university presidents reflect this new broadening of responsibilities involved with the job.

4

Job Classifications

Since teachers from kindergarten through college work with the youth of our nation, they share many problems and responsibilities. One and all, they deal with immature minds and emotions. They must guide in the making of decisions. They must introduce the growing girl or boy to the society in which she or he will have to find the way. Albert Einstein said, "It is the supreme art of the teacher to awaken joy in creative expression and knowledge."

General Duties of the Teacher

There is no particular age at which maturity is reached. We continue to mature all through our lives. Yet by the time a boy or girl graduates from high school, he or she takes a place among adults. Many high school students leave school to go to work. Of those students who graduate, the majority find jobs. Those who go on to college frequently live away from home.

This means that kindergarten, primary, junior, and senior high school teachers have one tremendous responsibility in common: the molding of the young. How does this affect their teaching?

State laws define the public school teacher's duties toward students as the obligation to maintain order and discipline over pupils and to teach effectively and efficiently. There is no explanation of just how the teacher is to perform the job effectively. In most states, this means following a state-approved course of study that recommends textbooks and materials.

Most of these materials are geared toward the average child. The teacher must realize that perhaps one-fourth of the class will be above average and one-fourth below. Moreover, average children can be different in temperament, interests, and goals. It is up to the teacher to understand the needs and requirements of each child and to see that each child's needs are met, at least in the classroom.

Kindergarten and Elementary School Teachers

According to the U.S. Bureau of the Census, public and private nursery school and kindergarten enrollments continue to grow with a new generation of baby boomers. Many kindergarten teachers will have more students, and many of these students will have attended preprimary school.

Elementary and kindergarten teachers usually have one group of pupils of the same grade for an entire term. They are responsible for the whole school program of that grade, and they teach all subjects. They often must supervise lunch periods and social programs and meet with parents, pupils, and other members of the teaching staff. In some schools, two or more teachers team-teach and are jointly responsible for a group of students or for a particular subject. More and more elementary school teachers now specialize in one or two subjects and teach these subjects to several classes.

The duties of elementary and kindergarten teachers are wide and varied, relating to all activities essential to the growth and development of young children. Teaching in the primary grades, therefore, is not a routine affair.

Teaching young children can be fun, but the teacher can also be the target of hostile feelings. The kindergarten and elementary teacher must be tactful, sympathetic, and understanding. The teacher must be alert to the relationships among the pupils and to their attitudes toward him or her as the adult leader. Many public elementary school teachers have aides who do clerical work and help supervise lunch and playground activities, freeing the teachers from these duties to devote more individual attention to students.

According to the National Association for the Education of Young Children, there has been an increased pressure by parents on the kindergarten teacher to make kindergarten more academic. While teachers have added science, computers, and even history to the curriculum, other plans include holding children back so they develop at their own pace to avoid burnout. Reading is increasingly being emphasized at the elementary schools.

Reading Instruction

The *Prepared to Make a Difference* 2000–03 research of the National Commission on Excellence in Elementary Teacher Preparation for Reading Instruction has recommended several ways to better prepare teachers at the undergraduate level to later contribute more effective teaching and learning of reading in elementary schools.

Findings include:

- Beginning teachers who graduated from quality programs are more successful and confident than their peers in making the transition into the teaching profession.
- These teachers are more effective in creating a rich literacy environment in their classrooms, both preparing students to read and engaging them in reading.
- Achievement in reading is higher for students who are engaged in the kinds of literacy activities that teachers from quality programs provide.

More information is available about the National Commission on Excellence in Elementary Teacher Preparation for Reading Instruction at the International Reading Association, 800 Barksdale Road, P.O. Box 8139, Newark, Delaware 19714-8139; pubinfo@ reading.org.

The Junior High School Teacher

The junior high school combines some of the qualifications and responsibilities of the elementary teacher with those of the high school teacher. Like their senior high school teacher colleagues, junior high school teachers specialize in the instruction of one subject. Unlike a senior high teacher, the teacher deals with younger boys and girls—ages eleven to fourteen.

As far as the teacher-student relationship is concerned, the job resembles that of the elementary school teacher. Junior high bridges the gap between childhood and adolescence. Its teachers face many of the elementary teacher's problems. They must be prepared for coping with children who are no longer babies but, on the other hand, are not completely able to take care of themselves. Since the junior high school teacher must at all times be aware of the adolescent problems of children, some background in child psychology is necessary.

To help students bridge the academic jump from elementary to high school, more and more teachers are developing courses that deal with particular areas within broad subjects. In this way students may acquire in-depth as well as general knowledge of a field.

The High School Teacher

In comparison with the elementary teacher, the high school teacher has a narrower range of duties, because he or she usually teaches only one or two subjects. The high school teacher also faces challenges vastly different from those on the elementary level. High school students are ready for more advanced knowledge and skills. They require more highly organized sports and more sophisticated social activities. The high school teacher is usually responsible for supervising some extracurricular program. This is, indeed, an important aspect of the job. Acting as a counselor, he or she helps organize all kinds of recreational clubs and social affairs and confers with students and their parents.

The high school teacher prepares examinations, keeps records, makes reports, and attends faculty meetings. Teachers also participate in activities such as workshops and college classes to keep up-to-date on their specialty subject and on current trends in education.

Developments in educational technology have provided teachers with instructional media and other new materials and techniques to improve student learning. The high school teacher must consider instructional methods that best meet the students' needs.

The Junior College Teacher

It is estimated that almost half of all students enrolled in two-year colleges are taking courses in occupational fields. Faculty trained in areas such as health technologies, business and data processing technologies, and public service fields may be in the most demand in the future. Since the institutions offer scores of job education programs in two years or fewer, there is likely to be considerable opportunity for persons trained to teach technical subjects requiring various kinds of skills.

Junior colleges have vocational, occupational, and technical courses that are designed to lead directly to employment in a specific established or emerging field. There are also programs geared to students who plan to continue their education at a four-year college or university. Teaching opportunities at junior colleges include arts and sciences and general studies, science or engineering-related occupational curricula, data processing technologies, health services, non-science- and non-engineering-related occupational curricula, business and commerce technologies, and public service technologies.

The College and University Teacher

Because the college teacher is dealing with a relatively mature adult, he or she has an entirely different responsibility from either the elementary teacher or the high school teacher. Basically, the job of the college teacher is to impart advanced knowledge through lectures or laboratory sessions. The college teacher is not normally concerned with the personality problems of the individual students or with the many other factors that face teaching colleagues in elementary or high schools. The most common subjects taught include social sciences, teacher education, the physical sciences, health professions, fine and applied arts, English, the biological sciences, mathematics, foreign languages, and business and commerce.

Generally speaking, there are two types of college teachers. The instructor in one of the professional fields, such as law, medicine, engineering, or education, is concerned with training graduate students in a specialty and thus concentrates on teaching the various aspects of one particular subject. The instructor in a liberal arts college also usually concentrates on one particular field, but the responsibility is broader in the sense that the students are interested in broad-based as well as technical education.

The college teacher's classroom responsibility is not as socially detailed as that of the elementary or high school teacher, although responsibilities will vary with college size and teacher personality. Students are expected to digest the teacher's precise information in class, but a teacher's responsibilities go beyond the class lecture. The college teacher is also expected to take an interest in the administration of the college's financial, academic, and social activities.

To be effective, college teachers must also keep up with research and developments in their field by reading current material, participating in professional activities, and conducting research. Many college teachers publish books and articles. In universities, about 70 percent of the faculty has published professional articles compared to 25 percent of two-year college faculty. In certain fields, such as engineering and the physical sciences, the demand for research is strong.

Many reports have cited low morale and a problem with commitment among college faculty at universities emphasizing research results rather than quality teaching. A study of 140 small liberal arts colleges, however, found that two-thirds of the faculty reported satisfaction and high morale at their schools due to "commitment to the missions of their colleges, a strong sense of community, and supportive leadership." The study, *Community, Commitment, and Congruence: A Different Kind of Excellence*, said that faculty at small liberal arts colleges expected to "have lengthy teaching careers" committed to regularly incorporating new knowledge into their teaching alternative outlets.

Salary

Teachers' salaries are constantly climbing. Although teachers have long been underpaid in comparison to other professionals, remuneration is starting to become proportionate to the importance of the job. This is largely due to teacher associations and an awakening by the community. But since taxpayers fund teachers' salaries, increases in pay lag behind those in privately owned companies.

Although at the present time there is a marked difference between the salary levels of high school and elementary school teachers, there is a growing trend toward equalizing them through a single-salary schedule. This equality means that, regardless of where teachers work, they will get equal pay based on their educational preparation. In other words, elementary, junior high, and senior high school teachers will get identical salaries if they hold the same degrees.

The single-salary schedule is supported by leading educational organizations that claim that it will go a long way to provide for better distribution of teachers between the elementary and high school levels. Thus, if you want to teach elementary school, you will get the same pay as a teacher on the high school level who has the same educational background and teaching experience as yourself.

The fixed salary schedules of almost all public school systems contain the following information:

- Starting pay for an entry-level position (bachelor's degree)
- Pay-scale increases, which are dependent upon longevity and further study or degrees
- Any additional increases of salary based upon cost of living or merit

Average Teacher Salaries

The average annual earnings of kindergarten, elementary, middle, and secondary school teachers ranged from $33,277 to $56,283 in 2002–03, according to an American Federation of Teachers (AFT) salary survey, which showed that there are concerted efforts to make education salaries more competitive with other professions, including better health insurance benefits whose costs had increased by 13 percent in 2002. Despite the relatively small salary growth, the average salaries for educators such as superintendents have grown as much as four times higher than average teachers' pay. The 2002–03 average teacher salary was $45,771, up 3.2 percent from $44,327 in 2001–02. The salary in the Virgin Islands was $24,764, Guam at $34,738, and Puerto Rico at $22,164, as estimated by the AFT 2002–03 survey. (See Table 4.1.)

Some of the findings include:

- California, Michigan, Connecticut, and New Jersey had the nation's highest average salaries in 2002–03.
- States in the lowest tier are South Dakota, Oklahoma, North Dakota, and Mississippi.

Table 4.1   Ten-Year Trend in Average Annual Salaries for Public School Classroom Teachers, 1994–2004

| School Year | Average Annual Classroom Teacher Salaries | | |
	Elementary	Secondary	All
1993–94	$35,233	$36,566	$35,737
1994–95	$36,088	$37,523	$36,675
1995–96	$37,138	$38,397	$37,642
1996–97	$38,039	$39,184	$38,443
1997–98	$39,002	$39,944	$39,350
1998–99	$40,079	$41,283	$40,533
1999–2000	$41,306	$42,546	$41,807
2000–2001	$42,911	$44,005	$43,378
2001–02	$44,200	$45,181	$44,632
2002–03	$45,627	$46,226	$45,891
2003–04	$46,712	$46,928	$46,826

Source: *Rankings and Estimates: Rankings of the States 2003 and Estimates of School Statistics 2004*, NEA Research, May 2004.

- In thirty-three states, 2002–03's base-salary level gains for teachers beat the 2.1 percent gain in the Employment Cost Index (a measure of compensation costs that includes wages, salaries, and employer costs for employee benefits). However, in the largest urban cities, the beginning salary grew just 1.6 percent in the same period. In 2002, more than half of all elementary, middle, and secondary school teachers belonged to unions—mainly the American Federation of Teachers and the National Education Association—that bargain with school systems over wages, hours, and other terms and conditions of employment. Fewer preschool and kindergarten teachers were union members—about 15 percent in 2002.

- In some schools, teachers getting a master's degree or national certification often results in a raise in pay, as does acting as a mentor. Some teachers earn extra income during the summer by teaching summer school or performing other jobs in the school system.

Beginning Teacher Salaries

Alaska had the highest average beginning salary in 2002–03 at $37,401. States joining Alaska in the top rank were New Jersey at $35,673, District of Columbia at $35,260, New York at $35,259, and California at $34,805. Montana had the lowest average beginning salary in 2002–03 at $23,052. The other states with low paying salaries included Maine at $24,631, South Dakota at $24,311, North Dakota at $23,591, and Arizona at $23,548. (See Table 4.2.)

Average Professor Salaries

Median annual earnings of all postsecondary teachers in 2002 were $49,040, according to Department of Labor statistics. The middle 50 percent earned between $34,310 and $69,580, with the lowest 10 percent earning less than $23,080 and the highest 10 percent earning more than $92,430. Earnings for college faculty vary according to rank and type of institution, geographic area, and field, according to a 2002–03 survey by the American Association of University Professors; salaries for full-time faculty averaged $64,455. The average was $86,437 for professors, $61,732 for associate professors, $51,545 for assistant professors, $37,737 for instructors, and $43,914 for lecturers. In fields with high-paying nonacademic alternatives—medicine, law, engineering, and business, among others—earnings exceeded these averages. In others—such as the humanities and education—they were lower.

In addition to their base salary, many faculty members realize significant earnings from consulting, teaching additional courses, research, writing for publication, or other employment. Part-time faculty members usually have fewer benefits than do full-time faculty.

Table 4.2 Actual Average Beginning Teacher Salaries 2002–03, Estimated 2004

	2002–03	2001–02		2003–04
Rank/State	Beginning Salary	Beginning Salary	% Change	Estimated Beginning Salary
1 Alaska	$37,401	$36,035*	3.8	$38,597
2 New Jersey	35,673[a]	35,311	1.0	36,815
3 District of Columbia	35,260	33,581*	5.0	36,388
4 New York	35,259[b]	32,549*	8.3	36,387
5 California	34,805[c]	34,180	1.8	35,919
6 Illinois	34,522[d]	31,761	8.7	35,627
7 Hawaii	34,000	32,000*	6.3	35,088
8 Georgia	33,919	32,561*	4.2	35,005
9 Delaware	33,811	32,868	2.9	34,893
10 Michigan	33,596[a]	32,649	2.9	34,671
11 Massachusetts	33,168[a]	32,746	1.3	34,230
12 Maryland	32,939	31,940*	3.1	33,993
13 Pennsylvania	32,897	31,866	3.2	33,950
14 Oregon	32,804	31,726*	3.4	33,854
15 Nevada	32,169	31,665*	1.6	33,198
16 Colorado	32,063	30,576*	4.9	33,089
17 Texas	31,874	30,938	3.0	32,894
18 Virginia	31,414[a, e]	31,238	0.6	32,420
19 Rhode Island	31,025[a]	30,272	2.5	32,018
20 Alabama	31,000	29,538*	4.9	31,992
21 Florida	30,491	29,733*	2.5	31,467
22 Louisiana	29,288	28,229	3.8	30,225
23 Indiana	29,144[e]	28,352*	2.8	30,077
24 Washington	29,118	28,348	2.7	30,050
25 Tennessee	29,045	28,074*	3.5	29,974
26 Ohio	28,866	27,484*	5.0	29,790
27 Connecticut	28,848	26,525*	8.8	29,771
28 Kentucky	28,886	26,813	7.7	29,770
29 South Carolina	28,672[f]	28,295*	1.3	29,590
30 Minnesota	28,600	27,400*	4.4	29,515
31 New Mexico	28,120[g]	27,579	2.0	29,020
32 Missouri	28,075	27,602*	1.7	28,973
33 Oklahoma	27,684	27,215*	1.7	28,570
34 North Carolina	27,572	27,572*	0.0	28,454

35 Wisconsin	27,277ʰ	27,397	−0.4	28,150
36 Utah	27,135ᵃ	26,806	1.2	28,003
37 Nebraska	27,127	26,010	4.3	27,995
38 Iowa	26,967	26,893*	0.3	27,830
39 Kansas	26,855ᵃ	26,596	1.0	27,714
40 New Hampshire	26,479	25,611	3.4	27,326
41 Mississippi	26,120	24,482*	6.7	26,956
42 Idaho	26,072	25,316	3.0	26,906
43 West Virginia	26,692	25,633	4.1	26,692ⁱ
44 Wyoming	25,694ᵃ	24,898*	3.2	26,516
45 Vermont	25,240	25,229	0.0	26,048
46 Arkansas	24,972	24,291*	2.8	25,771
47 Maine	24,631	24,054	2.4	25,419
48 South Dakota	24,311	23,938	1.6	25,089
49 North Dakota	23,591	22,004*	7.2	24,346
50 Arizona	23,548ʰ	24,972*	−5.7	24,302
51 Montana	23,052	22,344*	3.2	23,790

U.S. Average	$29,564	$28,661	3.2	$30,496
Difference 2002–03		$903		
% change			3.2	

Guam	$29,878	$29,878*	
Puerto Rico	18,000ʲ	18,000	
Virgin Islands	na	na	

* Note: These averages are based on revised data from state departments of education.

a AFT estimate
b Fifth percentile considered beginning salary
c Includes benefits where applicable
d Includes fringe benefits, pension pick-up, and extra-duty pay where applicable
e Includes supplemental pay
f Includes incentives
g Includes health insurance where applicable
h Includes extra-duty pay
i 2003–04 beginning salary provided by state department of education
j Figures from 2001–02

Source: American Federation of Teachers, *2003 Survey and Analysis of Teacher Salary Trends.*

Earnings for postsecondary career and technical education teachers vary widely by subject, academic credentials, experience, and region of the country. Part-time instructors usually receive few benefits.

Postsecondary Jobs

Postsecondary teachers held nearly 1.6 million jobs in 2002. Most were employed in public and private four-year colleges and universities and in two-year community colleges. Postsecondary career and technical education teachers employed by schools and institutes can specialize in training people in specific fields, such as technology centers or culinary schools. Some career and technical education teachers work for state and local governments and job training facilities. The following list shows postsecondary teaching jobs in specialties having twenty thousand or more jobs in 2002:

Graduate teaching assistants	128,000
Vocational education teachers	119,000
Health specialties teachers	86,000
Business teachers	67,000
Art, drama, and music teachers	58,000
English language and literature teachers	55,000
Biological science teachers	47,000
Education teachers	42,000
Mathematical science teachers	41,000
Nursing instructors and teachers	37,000
Computer science teachers	33,000
Engineering teachers	29,000
Psychology teachers	26,000

New Job Opportunities

Overall, employment of postsecondary teachers is expected to grow much faster than the average for all occupations through 2012, as projected by Department of Labor statistics. According to the report, a significant proportion of these new jobs will be part-time positions. Good job opportunities are expected as retirements of current postsecondary teachers and continued increases in student enrollments create numerous openings for teachers at all types of postsecondary institutions.

Projected growth in college and university enrollment over the next decade stems largely from the expected increase in the population of eighteen- to twenty-four-year-olds; adults returning to college and an increase in foreign-born students also will add to the number of students, particularly in the fastest-growing states of California, Texas, Florida, New York, and Arizona. Many new teachers will replace the large numbers of postsecondary teachers hired in the late 1960s and 1970s to teach the baby boomers, and they are expected to retire in growing numbers in the years ahead.

The number of earned doctorate degrees is projected to rise by only 4 percent over the 2002–12 period, sharply lower than the 10 percent increase over the previous decade. In spite of this positive trend, competition will remain tight for those seeking tenure-track positions at four-year colleges and universities, as many of the job openings are expected to be either part-time or renewable-term appointments. Job growth is expected to be strong over the next decade in teaching business, health specialties, nursing, and computer and biological sciences. Community colleges and other institutions offering career and technical education have rapidly increased, and these institutions are expected to offer some of the best opportunities for postsecondary teachers.

New Programs

A program called Preparing Future Faculty, administered by the Association of American Colleges and Universities and the Council of Graduate Schools, has created several independent programs that offer graduate students at research universities the opportunity to work as teaching assistants at other types of institutions, such as liberal arts or community colleges. Working with a mentor, the graduate students teach classes and learn how to improve their teaching techniques, make a curriculum, and balance the teaching, research, and administrative roles that faculty play.

Special publications such as *The Chronicle of Higher Education* list specific employment opportunities for faculty. For information on the Preparing Future Faculty program, contact: Association of American Colleges and Universities, 1818 R Street NW, Washington, D.C. 20009; aacu-ed.org.

Distance Learning

One sign of the times of the twenty-first century is the growing popularity of distance learning and online college study courses. These "virtual colleges" attract students who do not have either the time or the financial resources to attend college and who prefer "e-learning," through which one can earn degrees and even credits at the graduate level. At Miami-Dade College, for example, students took 7,612 online courses during the 2003 academic year, compared to 4,463 the previous year, according to school statistics. More than 4,000 Broward Community College students in Fort Lauderdale enrolled in ninety course sections provided entirely online in 2003, compared to 1998 when there were no online courses offered.

According to a report entitled *Thwarted Innovation: What Happened to E-Learning and Why* by a University of Pennsylvania research group, more community colleges and nontraditional universities have had success with distance learning, often with students enrolling in "blended" or "hybrid classes" that combine online study with in-class work as compared to traditional and big-name universities. The report said that "e-learning included a vision that learning would be 'customized, self-paced, and problem-based and that Web-facilitators might even replace professors,' but that did not happen." Internet tools like aol@school are being used for helping students and teachers for research and as a resource combined with classroom learning. (See Table 4.3.)

Business and Education

Business groups are continuously putting in skill and money to encourage teachers and students to better "invest" in education. For example, in June 2003, investment bankers Goldman Sachs Foundation and the Asia Society formulated an International Education Prize for Excellence in International Education to promote international knowledge and skills in both schools and in the community. The program annually awards five prizes of $25,000 each to teachers and their students in elementary schools, high schools, higher education institutions, and a private or nonprofit organization that have developed outstanding programs that use media/technology to educate students or teachers about other world regions and cultures.

The Asia Society has other education initiatives such as international studies, state initiatives, U.S.-China exchange, and classroom resources. The Asia Society is located at 725 Park Avenue, New York, New York 10021; internationalid.org.

Table 4.3 Number and Percentage Distribution of Two-Year and Four-Year Title IV Degree-Granting Institutions, by Distance Education Program Status and Institution Type and Size: 2000–2001

Institution Type and Size	Total Number of Institutions	Distance Education Program Status					
		Offered Distance Education in 2000–2001		Planned to Offer Distance Education in the Next 3 Years		Did Not Offer Distance Education in 2000–2001 and Did Not Plan to Offer in the Next 3 Years	
		Number	Percent	Number	Percent	Number	Percent
All institutions	4,130	2,320	56	510	12	1,290	31
Institution Type							
Public 2-year	1,070	960	90	50	5	50	5
Private 2-year	640	100	16	150	23	400	62
Public 4-year	620	550	89	20	3	50	8
Private 4-year	1,800	710	40	290	16	790	44
Size of Institution							
Less than 3,000	2,840	1,160	41	460	16	1,220	43
3,000 to 9,999	870	77	88	50	5	60	7
10,000 or more	420	400	95	10	2	10	2

Note: Percentages are based on the estimated 4,130 two-year and four-year Title IV degree-granting institutions in the nation. Detail may not sum to totals because of rounding.

Source: U.S. Department of Education, National Center for Education Statistics, Postsecondary Education Quick Information System (PEQIS) survey entitled *Distance Education at Higher Education Institutions, 2000–2001, 2002.*

Employment Conditions

Before you enter your teaching job, you should be fully aware of the conditions at the school. The enthusiastic new teachers in the book *The Blackboard Jungle* were horrified when they saw their visions of teaching disappear in the classroom "jungle." "I want to shape young minds, sculpt, create, let the students use their brains," comments one teacher in the book. Unfortunately, conditions would not allow it.

Before you start a new job in a school, you will need information—and the first day of school is not the right time to get it. During the orientation period and while speaking with experienced teachers at the school are the right times to get the feel of the school—not after you sign your contract.

Information may come from an administrator, from a supervisor, or from printed material the school releases. Although you might still feel inexperienced when you enter the classroom for the first time, at least knowing the employment conditions will give you more security.

Some of the following questions might be helpful to you in understanding the school's policies and conditions under which you will be working.

- Are there any basic school philosophies toward education, the community, school personnel, the children, or parents that I should know about?
- What are some unique things about the community that will help me become oriented to it? Can I get a city or area map?
- Is there a school directory and organizational chart available to me? Can I get a building chart that will show me the locations of administrative offices, the nurse, custodian,

restrooms, supply room, bulletin board for notices, audiovisual room?

- Does the school or system have a salary schedule, rules on tenure, retirement regulations?
- When is payday?
- What kind of housing will be available for me? What will it cost? Where is it located? Is it far from the school?
- Is there any insurance available to me and my family through the school—hospitalization, life insurance, retirement, accident?
- Does the school have a credit union?
- What are the provisions for sick leave, maternity leave, and absence with and without pay?
- Are there any specific requirements I should know about in case I need a substitute?
- Will I be able to participate in any in-service teachers' programs?
- What kinds of college or university courses are available to me in this vicinity?
- What are the provisions in this state and district regarding certification and renewal of certification?
- What are my teaching hours?
- Are there any special building policies related to food, smoking, and after-school use of facilities?

Mentoring

A sign of the times is the increasing use of mentors to help teachers progress through transitions. Veteran teachers are increasingly working as a team with new teachers to eliminate professional isolation.

Different mentoring programs for new teachers have proved helpful in getting them through the first year and, in turn, renewing enthusiasm for veteran teachers as they "view the profession through interns' fresh eyes." The Centerville, Ohio, Classroom Teachers Association, for example, in 2003 developed a program so successful that 96 percent of beginning teachers came back for a second year.

A National Education Association–Saturn/UAW Partnership award (which awards five schools annually) has developed mentoring programs jointly with local education associations. Teacher mentors go through three days of training and earn a stipend of $1,000. They also have a mentoring program to help experienced teachers new to the city or those who just need advice.

Various programs have been initiated to provide a support and buddy system for the beginning teacher around the country, ranging from the Pathwise Induction Program and the California Formative Assessment and Support System for Teachers (CFASST) to New Teacher Mentor Program and Ohio's Peer Assistance and Review (PAR).

CFASST helps teachers identify the methods of improving their practice with its motto, "Plan, Teach, Reflect, Apply."

The intern and mentor work together through the day and exchange feedback about classroom progress. The teams of young and old teacher together might remind one of police teams portrayed in popular movies, but teacher mentors do help ease the difficult early months.

"I thought I might be busy, but . . . it's like working three jobs," said one new teacher. "Yet my mentor showed me how to make things balance." One teacher said that team support from veteran teachers allows new teachers to teach their students in the best way possible.

The Teacher's Workload

Like many other professional workers, teachers go far beyond the traditional forty-hour week to meet the demands of their calling. The public is often misled by the relatively brief school day of pupils and has the mistaken idea that the teacher works short hours.

It is sometimes said that the teacher has easy hours, long vacations, and small teaching loads. This is not true. A recent survey of public school teachers indicated that the average teacher works 45.2 hours per week. However, when all extra teaching duties and tasks are taken into consideration, the total number of hours spent working each week was slightly more than 48, with about one-fifth of that time spent in unpaid activities, such as advising school clubs.

What do outside activities consist of? Grading and evaluating homework and tests, planning and preparing for each day's classes, and conferring with or about individual pupils are essential parts of the instructional services of the teacher. For the average teacher, these duties take half as much time as the class instruction itself, and they account for more than one-fourth of the total working time.

Correcting homework and class tests is a continuing task that averages 4.5 hours per week. The preparation of learning materials, personal study, and planning lessons all take time. Individual work with students outside class and conferences with parents also require much time.

There are other miscellaneous out-of-class assignments, including completing monitorial duties, keeping records, writing reports, attending faculty meetings, coaching, and sponsoring clubs.

Many teachers in large, medium, and small districts moonlight—that is, they have outside jobs. Some teachers have summer jobs, some have evening jobs, and others have weekend jobs. All teachers who have second jobs during the school year or who work during the summer are likely to work for an employer other than the school district. The tendency to take an additional job with the school is slightly stronger for metropolitan area teachers than for others. In these large school districts, there are more opportunities for a second school job.

Many teachers elect to teach during the summer. Others take jobs as camp counselors, private tutors, or writers. Sometimes, teachers conduct independent study projects during a vacation break. In many cases, a teacher can lead a foreign study group for travel in other countries. Many teachers earn additional income during the summer months by teaching summer school classes or tutoring.

Vacations for teachers are generally considered one of the best benefits. Many college terms end in late April or early May, giving teachers up to five months before the start of school in the fall. Secondary school teachers receive an average of two months of summer vacation. Winter breaks in colleges can give teachers up to six weeks. Weekends are always free unless the school has classes on Saturdays. All legal holidays are observed by schools as are the longer vacations at Christmas and Easter.

The average teaching day, from 9:00 A.M. to 3:00 P.M., is considered reasonable. During the school year, teachers work an average of 181 days. They average twenty-six teaching periods and five assigned periods a week. A new trend, split sessions and early classes that allow students to work during the day, requires classes to start as early as 7:15 A.M. in some cases.

In college teaching, the teaching load varies from school to school. Undergraduate faculty in four-year colleges and universities normally teach twelve hours a week and seldom more than fourteen or fifteen hours. Graduate faculties have teaching loads of about ten hours a week. Outside the classroom, teachers devote much time to preparation and other duties, averaging about forty hours a week on school-related activities.

A Department of Labor 2003 report found that three out of ten college and university faculty worked part-time in 2002. Some part-timers, who are sometimes known as "adjunct faculty," have primary jobs outside of academia—in government, private industry, or nonprofit research—and teach on the side. Many adjunct faculty are not qualified for tenure-track positions because they lack a doctoral degree.

A new sign of the times is technology—both a tremendous help but more work for the teacher. Requirements to teach online classes also have added greatly to the workloads of postsecondary teachers. Many find that developing the courses for the Internet online classes, in addition to learning how to operate the technology and answering large amounts of e-mail, has become very time-consuming. Internet, video conferencing, mobile phones, and other technical tools are a great boon but increase the time a teacher must communicate to students and colleagues and develop new interactive and continuously updated programs.

Community and junior college faculty generally teach twelve to seventeen hours a week. Often a college teacher can have a full schedule for three days a week and the other two days free. It is important to find out your working hours before you accept a teaching position.

Fringe Benefits

In addition to salary and time off, the following fringe benefits should also be taken into account.

Sick Leave

Almost every school system provides sick leave with full pay. The median number of days provided annually is ten. Ninety days is the median number of days that can be accumulated in school systems with student enrollments of twelve thousand or more.

Personal Leave

Increasing numbers of school systems provide a few days of leave a year with pay for urgent personal reasons, such as sickness or death in the immediate family, religious holidays, jury duty, and court summons.

Sabbatical Leave

Sabbaticals for study, travel, or recuperation of health, although common in colleges and universities, are offered in only a small number of other school systems. Typical payment during sabbatical leave is one-half of full salary. Colleges usually grant a sabbatical leave after six or seven years of employment.

Insurance

Many school systems and teacher organizations offer one or more types of insurance either completely paid for, partially paid for, or at group rates paid for by the individual teacher. Types of insurance include group health insurance, including hospitalization; group life insurance, usually term insurance; and liability insurance to cover possible liability arising from student injuries.

Extra Pay

In some schools, teachers receive supplementary pay for certain school-related activities, such as coaching students in sports and working with students in music, dramatics, school publications, or other extracurricular activities.

Retirement Benefits

The local teacher's organization will probably have a list of all the benefits the school offers. All states have retirement programs for public school teachers. Often, large cities have their own schedules. Systems usually vary from one plan to another, but according to several sources, these are representative provisions of retirement plans:

- Teachers contribute about 5 percent of their salaries, which is automatically deducted from their pay. The state or school system contributes at least a similar amount.
- Benefits paid to teachers upon retirement depend upon years of service and age at retirement.
- A frequent objective is to provide retirement benefits at age sixty-five, after thirty to thirty-five years of service, equal to one-half of the average earnings during the last, or highest, five to ten years of earnings.
- Except for Social Security, there is practically no transfer of retirement fund credits from one state or city to another.
- A teacher who leaves a state or city retirement system may usually take with him or her all contributions paid into the retirement system, but he or she is not credited with employer's contributions.

- Many retirement plans allow early retirement before the age sixty-five at a reduced benefit.
- Often the retirement plan also provides payment in case of disability before retirement and survivor's benefits in case of death.

In anticipation of an oversupply of teachers, new retirement packages have been offered to teachers in the past few years. But as the demand for teachers has increased, some states, like Texas, now offer retired teachers jobs with their pensions remaining, and that might signify a trend. Each state varies in its benefits, and the Teachers Insurance and Annuity Association-College Retirement Equities Fund (TIAA-CREF) is being advocated for public school teachers. As many states are now experiencing a shortage of teachers, teachers who move to new employment in another state will be negotiating their contracts to keep the credit accrued toward retirement.

Other

College and university teachers may also enjoy certain benefits, including tuition waivers for dependents, housing allowances, travel allowances, and leaves of absence.

Rural Versus Urban Teaching

Where you teach is important to you. Every area differs in temperament and school policies. You must decide which you prefer: rural or urban teaching. There are advantages and disadvantages in both areas.

Very often teachers tend to remain in the community in which they grew up and teach in their local schools. If a man or woman is brought up in the rural section of Kentucky, for example, he or she is likely to become a teacher in the school that he or she attended. By the same token, if a person attended a high school in Los Angeles, he or she may not want to leave the city when ready to teach.

Surveys indicate that rural schools search constantly for an adequate supply of competent teachers, administrators, and supervisors. Thus more opportunities are found in rural areas than in the highly competitive urban centers. However, since rural areas are financially less able to support their schools than are wealthier urban districts, their schools lag far behind the city schools in pay scales.

Despite your choice, some states will not admit persons from other states, even though they may hold teaching licenses from recognized colleges, unless they take more courses and obtain a new license to teach in that state.

You should evaluate the merits of city and rural areas. Where would you be happier living and working? Where would you have the greatest opportunity for advancement? In which setting would you like to teach? These are but a few questions that come to mind.

Rural Teaching

"Rural teaching was creative," says Mrs. Darrie Walden, who taught school from 1910 to 1954 in small towns in Florida. "After the fall harvest, I had about thirty children from beginners to fifth grade. Every child owned his own book or books. Teaching materials were big picture charts with words or short sentences. . . . The school had outdoor toilets, and the children drew water from an open spring.

"In the thirties, most of my teaching was from the chalkboard. About thirty pupils in grades seven and eight used my set of books and three sets the trustees bought for the school."

Reminiscing about happy times in the schools, Mrs. Walden recalled softball games, spelling bees, picnics, and farmers bringing the school supplies of peas, beans, and ripe tomatoes. Explaining why she stayed in rural teaching, Mrs. Walden says, "I dedicated my life in the early part of my teaching to rural children. Salaries were small, but it didn't cost much to live. Salary was not the motivation. It was love for children and underprivileged people."

Some of the advantages of rural teaching include the following:

- You can advance faster and gain academic recognition more easily.
- As a rural teacher, you will have greater prestige and respect in your community.
- You will find living costs less expensive.
- You will find it easier to enter into the social life of the community.

Some disadvantages of rural teaching include the following:

- Your salary will be lower than it would be in the city.
- The building in which you teach is liable to be in poorer condition.
- You may find your equipment and supplies to be inadequate.
- Laboratory and library facilities in the school and in the community itself may be inadequate.

- You may find that your personal life is more limited by the community.

Urban Teaching

The following are some advantages of city teaching:

- City or suburban teachers usually receive higher salaries.
- The buildings, supplies, and equipment are usually better in the city.
- The city offers more cultural opportunities in the way of museums, operas, shows, libraries, and similar facilities.
- There is less interference with your personal life in the city.

The following are disadvantages of city teaching:

- There is less opportunity for advancement.
- The schools are big and the atmosphere impersonal.
- There is less chance of getting a job.
- There may be higher standards for certification.
- It may be difficult to get close to pupils or parents because of the size of the school and community.

As you can see, there are arguments for and against both city and rural teaching. In the last analysis, you will have to make the decision for yourself.

Advantages and Disadvantages of Teaching

What makes a person decide on teaching as a career? What advantages does he or she expect from the job? What does teaching offer that no other profession can give?

In one study by Fritz Redl and William Wattenburg, teachers were asked why they went into the field. Many different reasons were stated:

- Status
- Family pressure
- Love for subject matter
- Identification with a former teacher
- Love of children
- Fun in teaching
- Helping to build a better world
- Self-sacrifice
- Reliving childhood patterns
- Desire for affection
- Need for power
- Guaranteed superiority

Advantages

- **Working with young people.** A large number of men and women enjoy working with youngsters. You may find that you have a genuine knack for working with children and that the experience is enjoyable as well as highly revealing. Many children, who are less inhibited than adults, make you aware of the kind of person you are. One of the most positive aspects of teaching is that while you help others to grow, you also grow.
- **The fun of teaching.** Teaching offers you constant diversity and an opportunity to experiment. Helping people learn is an exciting job that will utilize your inventiveness, your sympathy, and your understanding of the social world and the particular problems of the children you teach. What is more, the teaching profession provides, in most states, for periodic leaves of absence for further pro-

fessional study or for travel. Foreign exchange teaching makes possible additional opportunities for experience.

• **Community respect.** For the most part, teachers, next to ministers, are the most respected members of their communities. They are looked up to as community leaders. As a teacher, you will be called upon frequently to lead in intellectual discussions at town forums or parents' meetings. You will be asked to help in various programs that may take place in your town or city. You will get prestige in being a teacher—prestige that is not measured in dollars and cents.

Sometimes, though, the community neglects its teachers. Sometimes, too, the teacher must lead a restricted personal life. But that attitude is rapidly changing. Teachers are now accepted as persons in the community who can be counted upon at all times to serve their fellow citizens when such help is needed. This is an intangible compensation that makes teaching worthwhile.

• **Retirement plans.** An important advantage of the teaching profession is that today every state has a retirement plan. The existence of a retirement plan in an occupation gives the worker peace of mind and a sense of security for the future. When you reach the age of sixty-five or seventy and can no longer teach, you are not left without resources. There are now some early retirement plans that are based on the length of teaching experience. Teachers can retire at as young as fifty years old. The school system, through its retirement program, will take care of you.

• **Tenure.** Teaching offers another important compensation—a majority of the nation's teachers now have tenure. Under tenure, you cannot be fired unless you are involved in something illegal or are found incompetent. It is a great security for teachers.

• **Classroom hours.** In addition to the long vacations, teachers have a pleasant arrangement for their classroom teaching. The average teacher is in class six hours a day, five days a week. Of course, the day does not end there.

Aside from these specific advantages, teachers in general find their work interesting, challenging, and creative, affording them an opportunity to earn a living in a field of special interest to them and giving them the immense satisfaction of being an important factor in the physical, moral, and intellectual development of young people.

Disadvantages

Aside from such general considerations as low rate of pay, personal restrictions in some localities, poor teaching facilities, heavy workloads, monotony, and out-of-class work responsibilities, many of the conditions that may be considered disadvantages may or may not be such, depending on your personality.

Who you are as a person will determine your happiness and success in teaching. If you are a mature, emotionally healthy person, you will expect certain irritations that are part of living itself and that exist in all human relations—whether you are a teacher, a nurse, or any other kind of worker. These irritations may be considered disadvantages by certain individuals who cannot overcome them and are thus frustrated by them.

For instance, your ability to become an integral part of the life of your school and to live in harmony with your fellow teachers is an important one. Certain teachers may be unfriendly to you; some may act superior; the principal, department head, or other school administrator may do things or issue orders with which you disagree. All of these things require stability on your part and the ability to adapt yourself to such conditions.

You may be saddled with an unusual amount of clerical detail that is not really your job. You may feel defeated and fear that your talents are not appreciated. But here again a healthy outlook and a broad viewpoint will help you adjust to the temporary inconvenience. There may be days when you have a headache or are just not in the mood to cope with thirty-five exuberant youngsters.

When you have to face problems or when you feel resentment toward job or classroom duties, view things in their proper perspective. If you are abrupt with a student for no apparent reason, question your motives. Maybe the fault lies with you.

The Association for Childhood Education International says the following in summing up the advantages and disadvantages of teaching:

- Teachers do not make much money, but their jobs are usually stable and secure.
- Teachers spend long hours outside the classroom making preparation, sponsoring clubs or sports, working with faculty committees, helping in community projects; but these undertakings contribute to the teachers' effectiveness in the classroom and help them to become valued and responsible citizens of the community.
- Teachers live in a goldfish bowl of community attention and gossip, but they have many pleasant social contacts.
- Some teachers become bossy when they spend so much time with younger people, but most teachers delight in the success of their pupils.
- Teaching is monotonous work for some, but for others, it is highly individual, creative, and responsible.
- Teaching is hard work, but it is work that makes a difference in the lives of boys and girls and, ultimately, in the future of the nation.

Teachers themselves cite disadvantages of the profession including stagnation, children getting out of hand, and isolation.

How can we sum up the advantages of teaching? Perhaps in this way: good teachers receive great professional satisfaction from working with their students, their colleagues, and the public to advance the objectives of democracy and American education.

The First Year

Many teachers give up within their first five years of teaching. According to statistics, there is an estimated 30 percent attrition rate in the first five years, with almost 50 percent in urban and isolated rural areas. The costs can take a toll.

To counter the often demoralizing first year, the booklet *What to Expect Your First Year of Teaching* by Amy DePaul goes straight to the source—award-winning first-year teachers. They offer guidance through their own experiences during this tumultuous period.

"I tried to create a nurturing, educational, and safe environment for these students," commented third- and fourth-grade teacher Scott D. Niemann from Alaska. "Teaching wasn't only my job, it was fast becoming my lifestyle."

The Department of Education through the Sallie Mae Corporation provides funding and support for education loans and sponsors an annual award for first-year teachers. They gather the winners in Washington, D.C., to discuss issues that affected them the most. Other new programs are encouraging teachers to "keep up" and not "give up" by providing both financial and moral support.

5

RELATED FIELDS

THERE ARE MANY opportunities to grow in the field of education. It is true that the majority of all workers are regular classroom teachers, but there are also many specialized fields related to teaching.

Teachers involved in the area of constant learning have regular opportunities to work in related fields. As a consultant, research worker, or perhaps a Defense Department appointee, the teacher is presented with many opportunities outside the classroom.

Those entering the teaching profession are also qualified for other jobs if there is a job scarcity. When there is a depletion of regular teaching jobs, a teacher can seek a related job in the field of education or utilize the strengths of the teaching profession to go to other professions.

Many teachers regard the teaching experience as a way of eliciting a spark from within themselves and providing background for other professions. Maria Montessori, the gifted Italian educator who developed a system of early education, says in the book *The Absorbent Mind*:

We find ourselves confronted by a child no longer to be thought of as helpless, like a receptive void waiting to be filled with our wisdom . . . but one guided by his inward teacher. We teachers can only help the work going on, as servants wait upon a master. We then become witnesses to the development of the human soul; the emergence of the New Man, who will no longer be the victim of events . . . but will become able to direct and to mold the future of mankind.

Nontraditional Education Opportunities

A teacher has many duties and is many things. A good teacher is a psychologist, a generalist in many fields, and a humanist who cares deeply about people. Because teacher training aims to develop inquiring minds and because it stresses individual growth, it is a starting point for many kinds of careers, both in teaching and in other fields.

Starting Your Own School

Teachers, with their broad knowledge of psychology and understanding of youth, have often established excellent private schools. Caring for and teaching preschool children is extremely important in this era of working mothers. Many enterprising young teachers have initiated popular schools for preschool children. Other teachers have founded private schools based on their own interpretations of teaching.

Private Tutoring

You can, if you wish, earn money through private tutoring. Teachers are frequently called upon to help tutor students who are not able to grasp a subject in the classroom. This interesting type of work can be done on a part-time basis after school or in the evening. Several teachers have left teaching jobs to open successful private tutoring businesses of their own. Many teachers specialize in preparing students for standardized tests such as the SAT. Some teachers specialize in tutoring foreign students who will take examinations in medicine or law. Teachers always have the opportunity to be self-employed by teaching the skills they know best.

Speech Consultant

Because teaching requires you to speak in front of your class, you should learn how to be at ease with public speaking. This attribute can prove valuable if you are interested in entering the field of speech consultant work. Some teachers associate themselves with groups who teach people how to speak properly and effectively. Others have opened their own speech clinics and have been quite successful in this work.

Vocational-Technical Education

As technology becomes more involved, there is a great need for teachers to instruct workers. Teaching certificates are not always required. The Education Professions Development Act has instituted a program between the states and industry to allow skilled technicians to teach part-time in the schools. The instructor's up-to-date knowledge is useful to the school, and he or she may gain the teaching skills necessary to meet state certification.

Vocational-technical education teachers usually must have the proper licenses or certificates to teach full-time in schools. Often work experience is credited toward a degree. Veterans and retired military personnel also get credit for training they have received.

Counselors in the field of vocational-technical education usually have master's degrees and state certification. Curriculum specialists and other school personnel also need at least a bachelor's degree to qualify for a job, although they do not need state certification.

Early Childhood Education Careers

Although there is an adequate supply of primary teachers, the field of preschool education is expanding. Besides the field of preschool child care centers, there are special jobs in early childhood education. For children ages six through nine, there are reading specialists to help diagnose learning disabilities and curriculum specialists to help plan studies.

An increasing number of young students are now going into the classroom at three and four years old, and the number of students keeps growing. This means an increased need for preschool teachers. Preschool teachers filled 842,000 teaching positions in 2001, working in school-based and business-based child care centers. Often teachers are not required to have full education credits to teach at these schools. But increased numbers of youngsters preparing for kindergarten means preschool teachers who expected not only to supervise play but also to develop a sense of fair play within the student. Professional opportunities for teaching in preschool programs are expected to increase at a higher-than-average rate through 2005.

Substitute Teaching

Substitute teachers are increasingly receiving more money and benefits as the demand for their services grows. The Substitute Teaching Institute at Utah State University estimated that from kindergarten to high school graduation, students spend a full year with substitutes. Different unions such as the NEA and AFT affil-iates are bargaining for increased salaries and benefits. A govern-ment survey of large school districts estimated that average substitute pay was $87.50 a day in the 2002–03 school year. In other school districts, like Los Angeles, substitutes make $156 a day or $211 after twenty-one days. Those who work one hundred days a year get full health insurance the following year. As the role of substitute teachers is increasing, some unions have put training for substitutes into their contract, like the NEA-affiliated Wisconsin Education Association Council course, founded in 1996; an online course is also available. For more information on substitute teach-ing contact nea.org/substitutes, substituteteachers.org, and the National Substitute Teachers alliance at nstasubs.org.

Teacher Aides

One of the largest-growing groups in the United States labor force is teacher aides. Due to the growing pressure and diversity of teach-ers' duties, having teacher assistants in the classroom has become more necessary. Often teacher aides later become teachers by con-tinuing their education.

Those wishing to work as teacher aides or paraprofessionals must have permits or certificates in some states. Other states require aides to have a minimum number of semester hours of college study and experience in children's education. The U.S. Department of Edu-cation has published a suggested standard curriculum for assistants consisting of thirteen courses, which, combined with work in the classroom—either as assistants or during a practical course for full-time students—leads to an associate's degree.

Teacher assistants were first introduced into schools for economic reasons to make up for the shortage of qualified teachers and make more efficient use of the materials and human resources of schools. They are increasingly being used in special fields such as bilingual teaching, teaching children of immigrants or minority groups, and special education. Although most assist at the primary level, those working in secondary schools may perform more technical activities, such as audiovisual work and laboratory maintenance.

The Department of Labor estimated that there were 1.3 million teacher assistant jobs in 2002, with three out of four working at state and local schools and the rest at private institutions. The California Projections of Employment, published by the Labor Market Information Division of the Employment Development Department, projected that the number of teacher aides in California will reach 217,250 by 2005, an increase in new jobs of 61,380 since 1993. There will also be an estimated 32,500 job openings due to people retiring or leaving the occupation. Added to the 61,380 new jobs expected, this makes for an estimated total of 93,880 job opportunities through 2005.

Beginning salaries for most teacher aides are between minimum wage and $11.50 an hour. With some experience, teacher aides may earn from the minimum to $13.00 per hour. Some school districts pay slightly higher wages to aides working in special education programs. Teacher aides in these programs experience a high turnover rate because they find that work with mentally and physically disabled students may be too difficult or challenging for them.

A survey of assistants in state schools in Minneapolis found that by using assistants, teachers gained an average of seventeen extra hours per week to devote to students. Other evaluations on programs using assistants in New York and Florida showed that aides teaching low-income parents how to contribute to better educating their children enabled these children to progress better than non-tutored children from the same environment.

Although European teacher associations are not enthusiastic about using teacher aides, the National Education Association and the American Federation of Teachers (AFT) have given their total support to the utilization of assistants. The AFT accepts them as full members.

"We should prepare educators to respond to the wide variety of students who now attend our schools—students who learn in different ways, speak different languages, and bring cultural values to the classroom," state authors John Goodlad and Pamela Keating in the book *Access to Knowledge: An Agenda for Our Nation's Schools.*

Special Education

Special education is one of the fastest-growing professions, expected to increase much faster than the average for all occupations through 2012. Rapid employment and job turnover, coupled with continued increases of special education students needing services, legislation emphasizing training and employment for individuals with disabilities, and educational reforms requiring higher standards for graduation, are expected to result in a favorable job market.

The various types of disabilities delineated in government special education programs include specific learning disabilities, mental retardation, speech or language impairment, serious emotional disturbance, visual and hearing impairment, orthopedic impairment, autism, traumatic brain injury, and multiple disabilities. Special education teachers are legally required to help develop an Individualized Education Program (IEP) for each special education student.

Requirements for special education teachers start with a bachelor of arts degree from a school offering a program in special education. The master's degree and doctorate could be useful for advancement. Certification requirements vary from state to state. Some states require a bachelor's degree in education or special education for certification, while others require a master's degree in special education for permanent certification. Educators of the physically and mentally disabled must be excellent teachers sensitive to the feelings of the children.

Median annual earnings in 2002 of special education teachers who worked primarily in preschools, kindergartens, and elementary schools were $42,690, similar to the median annual earnings of middle school special education teachers at $41,350. The average annual earnings of special education teachers teaching primarily in secondary schools were $44,130. In 2002, about 62 percent of special education teachers belonged to unions—mainly the American Federation of Teachers and the National Education Association—that bargain with school systems over wages, hours, and the terms and conditions of employment.

Gifted

Some fifteen states now require that teachers of the gifted complete graduate courses that specifically relate to teaching gifted students. The Council for Exceptional Children offers information on some of the shortages that now exist in teaching. Areas of demand include special education teacher aides, teachers of the gifted, child psychologists, diagnosticians, speech pathologists or audiologists, occupational or physical therapists, teachers of the deaf, and teachers of the blind. Administrators, supervisors, and researchers for state, local, and institutional activities are also needed.

Teachers of gifted children always require good teacher training. Special schools for the gifted have established studies to allow the student to progress to his or her own level without being restricted by a steadfast curriculum. The U.S. Department of Education has established an office dealing with bright and artistically talented students to help coordinate government aid for the gifted.

Other opportunities in special education exist for therapists in recreation and music, social workers, child development specialists, occupational and physical therapists, child care specialists, speech and hearing specialists, psychometricians, and visual specialists. These specialists work in regular and special schools, residential schools, hospitals, treatment centers, or students' homes.

Coordinators are needed to administer agreements between schools and vocational rehabilitation centers, between schools and hospitals, and between two schools. Other special education jobs include arranging for artists to perform for handicapped students or bringing students to special events. A dance teacher, for example, can incorporate teaching dance and pantomime to deaf students.

More information on special education can be found at the National Clearinghouse for Professions in Special Education, Council for Exceptional Children, 1920 Association Drive, Reston, Virginia 20191.

Self-Enrichment

According to the Department of Education, opportunities for jobs as adult literacy, remedial, and self-enrichment education teachers are expected to grow more rapidly than all the education occupations through 2012. The report has found that the burgeoning need for self-enrichment teachers can be attributed to the growing number of people of a wide variety of ages embracing lifelong learning. Subjects that are not easily researched on the Internet and those that provide hands-on experiences, such as cooking, crafts, the arts, yoga, spirituality, and self-improvement, are projected to be in greater demand. Median hourly earnings of self-enrichment teachers were $14.09 in 2002, and median hourly earnings of adult literacy, remedial education, and GED teachers and instructors were $17.50.

English as a Second Language

Significant employment growth is anticipated especially for teachers of English as a Second Language (ESL). These teachers will be needed by the increasing number of immigrants and other residents living in this country who need to either learn or enhance their skills in English. Minorities like the Chinese, Koreans, Indians, and other non-English-speaking groups also are developing their own schools, thus requiring teachers of English.

Kathleen Mellor, the NEA Teacher of 2004, is an ESL teacher at North Kingston, Rhode Island, who found the work a "partnership between the mainstream teachers and ESL teachers to integrate the students into the system." Demand for ESL teachers is estimated to be the greatest in states such as California, Florida, Texas, and New York, due to their large populations of residents who have limited English skills. However, the Department of Labor has found that parts of the Midwest and Plains states have begun to attract large numbers of immigrants, making for especially good opportunities in those areas as well.

Ethnic Teaching

Minority populations in the country are in great need of bilingual education and ethnic studies relating to their own backgrounds. Teachers are needed who can speak foreign languages and can translate elementary and secondary school life into the mainstream of Latino, Native American, or Asian life. Many students attend schools outside their own neighborhoods. Teachers are needed who are familiar with different ethnic cultures and who can wipe away old generalizations about different nationalities.

In the 1960s and 1970s, institutions responded to increased numbers of minority students by forming separate counseling and support programs. More recently the trend has been to integrate these services into broader efforts to improve the academic preparation of all students needing help. Minorities will make up nearly 40 percent of all eighteen- to twenty-four-year-olds by the year 2025, according to the report *Focus on Minorities: Trends in Higher Education Participation and Success.*

Minority participation in higher education has declined significantly, although enrollment of Asian-Americans has increased in recent years. The number of Latino youth in higher education has continued to decline because of their failure to complete high school. This calls for teachers with a greater awareness of the changing population and curricula oriented to special groups.

Latino television, newspaper publishing, and other services geared to the Latino community are encouraging the new generation to be educated in both English and Spanish to achieve in this new, expanding arena. "Bilingual education and English learning is one of the most vital areas of interaction between teacher and student to achieve communication," said Jose Luis Nazar, founder and CEO of Lexicon, a pioneering Los Angeles–based English teaching program geared for the Latino community. "The constant growth of Hispanic and other communities will find that the teachers of English will be their most important link to America."

Thirty years ago the Puerto Rican Legal Defense Fund sued and won a consent decree requiring that New York City offer bilingual education. Since then, bilingual education has been conceived as a virtual civil right for Latinos in New York City and around the country. A new trend is English-immersion classes, which is based on findings in 1994 and 2000 that "children qualified for mainstream classes more rapidly coming from ESL programs than from bilingual education in the students' native language." A school in Brooklyn served as a test model of a compromise between ESL and bilingual education of what the New York Department of Education calls "improvement of teacher training and performance standards."

Audiovisual Specialists

Audiovisual specialists are men and women who translate educational ideas into films, photographs, digital images, videotapes, DVDs, tape recordings, slides, and other teaching tools. Audiovisual (AV) specialists work with machines that supplement classroom instruction. These specialists usually work in media centers maintained by school districts for use by schools within the system.

Educational Television Specialists

The educational television specialist in this rapidly expanding field combines education and broadcasting to include such responsibilities as planning and writing programs, conducting program research, designing television classes, and writing materials. Teachers who are interested in film and broadcasting may find this a perfect combination of classroom and communication.

Internet and Technology Education

The Internet and further use of technology is projected to change many of the fundamental ways of teaching and learning. There are various Internet services that seek teachers to formulate programming and do long-distance teaching.

Some of the websites that show the varied applications of teaching on the Internet include Alliance for Global Learning, which networks educational projects; Blueprint for Interactive Classrooms, a distance-teaching classroom; Community Share Week, which invites classrooms to create and launch a Web page to highlight their activities and use in their classroom curriculum; World Links for Development, which links students and teachers in secondary schools in developing countries with students and teachers in industrialized countries for collaborative learning programs via the Internet; Interactive Distance Learning Group, a consortium of industrial companies with interactive training and education courses via satellite with audio and data feedback; and Site Alive, which links the classroom to students at field sites around the world.

Adult Education

The Adult Education Association of the United States, founded in 1951, provides information, publications, and services in this field of education. Teachers interested in teaching specialized subjects, such as learning for the aged, "how to" classes, and other diversified subjects, can contact churches, schools, and organizations to see what adult education courses are offered. Teaching adult education classes is often an excellent opportunity for retired teachers who do not want to withdraw entirely from the classroom. As more adults enroll in continuing education classes—either for career advancement, career-change skills, or personal interest—the need for adult education teachers will increase. The National Center for Education Statistics *Condition of Education 2004* report found that

40 percent of the population age sixteen and above participated in some work-related adult education in 2002–03. The most common types of programs were formal work-related courses and college or university degree programs for work-related reasons.

Holocaust Studies

The teaching of history and literature of the Holocaust has become a specialized area in both high school and higher education courses. Awards like the Yavner Award provide funds for teachers in New York who make "outstanding contributions to teaching about the Holocaust and other violations of human rights."

School Volunteer

At a recent conference of school volunteers and aides, many of these workers expressed their kinship with teachers. Many volunteers begin on this level and progress to becoming teachers after seeing the rewards of the profession. Volunteers tutor and do the things teachers and staff members do not have time to complete. Some teachers also volunteer their time, such as a Los Angeles music teacher who comes to an elementary school to teach every week. The principal of the school said that there would be no music programs were it not for the volunteers.

Public Lecturing

Many teachers and professors who are acknowledged authorities in their fields are called upon to lecture before public gatherings. These lecturers can, and often do, command a fee. For those who want to get out of teaching and enter their own business, setting up a lecture bureau is a possibility. The training you get in teaching helps you meet people, talk freely, and make the contacts necessary to undertake a business of this kind. However, there are many pitfalls, and the field should be surveyed thoroughly before beginning a project of this nature. There is also the possibility of serving as a consultant or in an advisory capacity with an established lecture firm. Teachers always have the security of going back to their classrooms if the lecture circuit becomes frenzied or unrewarding.

Music Instruction

If you are musically talented, you can supplement your teaching income by giving music lessons. Many music teachers earn substantial sums by building up a private music practice. Teachers can conduct a student symphony, play in an orchestra, and tutor. Some teachers have opened up their own music shops or have maintained these shops on a part-time basis. Other areas of art also may be taught part-time, including dance, photography, painting, and other creative subjects.

Administration and Business

The knowledge and skills teachers possess are valued in a number of different areas and translate well to the needs and requirements of the business world in particular.

Personnel Work

Many teachers go from teaching into industry and business as personnel directors. Business leaders want and need people who can judge which people are suited to which kinds of jobs and who are capable of training personnel and dealing with morale problems. Teaching experience helps people develop this sense of judgment.

Government Work

The need for administrative details and specialized knowledge by government agencies has created a need for many teachers. Many top universities have their best professors called to Washington. Dr. Henry Kissinger, a former Harvard professor who became secretary of state, is a good example of a professor being called to apply theories to the world of politics. Since President John Kennedy searched the nation's campuses for talent, no political leader has ignored the country's teachers.

Business Consultants

Some business corporations, under special fellowship programs, invite professors to work in their offices three months a year. The remuneration is high, and working in business is good opportunity for business professors to get practical experience and learn the latest business practices to aid teaching effectiveness in the classroom.

Executive Secretaries to Professional Groups

This is a little-understood but important field of activity for teachers. Almost every major local, state, or national organization has an executive secretary to coordinate its work. These secretaries are usually paid; large state or national groups hire them full-time. Often by starting from a volunteer position, a person can be placed on the payroll and progress even further in the education field.

Camp Work

A teacher's long summer vacation allows time to engage in a private business. Summer camps provide a good outlet for the business-minded teacher who enjoys children. Parents, too, usually have more confidence in a camp staffed by teachers. Each summer, thousands of teachers work in camps as counselors, guidance directors, physical education instructors, or any one of a number of positions commonly found in a camp. Moreover, many teachers now own summer camps and operate them as profitable ventures. The teacher-operated camps have proved successful, both financially and educationally.

Radio and Television

In addition to educational television, teachers can often participate in other fields of radio and television. Teachers may find part-time jobs in broadcasting or in presenting programs. "The reason why I'm such a good host and questioner," commented one radio host, "is because I'm a former teacher and used to asking my students pointed questions."

TV and radio stations are also increasing on campus. George Schwartz, for example, started the first classical music FM radio station in the Philadelphia area with his students at the Mercer County Community College in Trenton, New Jersey.

Film

Film and teaching often blend together. Opportunities abound for teachers who also have practical experience. Often books, documentaries, and student films are being produced by film teachers,

and film instructors have become important in shaping the future
Academy Award–winning director.

Instructional Coordinators

Instructional coordinators, also known as curriculum specialists,
staff development specialists, or directors of instructional material,
must have a good understanding of how to teach specific groups of
students and train teachers in addition to expertise in developing
and standardizing educational materials. They also assist in implementing new technology in the classroom such as Internet software
and often specialize in specific subjects such as reading, language
arts, and mathematics or curriculum development. Many instructional coordinators are former teachers or principals, and a minimum educational requirement for instructional coordinators is a
bachelor's degree, usually in education with a master's or higher
degree preferred. Instructional coordinators held about ninety-eight
thousand jobs in 2002 working in education, individual and family
services, scientific research, and development services. Median
annual earnings of instructional coordinators in 2002 were $47,350.

Writing

Given their intimate knowledge of certain subject areas and their
ability to impart this knowledge to others, many teachers naturally
find a place in careers that require strong writing and communi-
cating skills.

Public Relations

This is a field that requires a combination of good common sense
and the ability to understand and get along with people. Teaching

can prove a good foundation for work in public relations. It helps people speak and write clearly and develop poise in the presence of others.

Textbook Writing

Millions of dollars are spent each year on the purchase of textbooks of all kinds. For the most part, textbooks are written by teachers and educators. Some teachers have earned enough money to be able to retire as a result of their textbook writing. Of course, you need to be a specialist in some field, whether it is in the project method in kindergarten, the subject of algebra in high school, or American history in college. If you like to write books, teaching will give you a good start, and the background you get in school will serve you later on in your career. A scholar never stops learning, and writing often helps one to review and better define a subject. Of course, the idea of "publish or perish" in some schools speeds a professor to write.

Newspaper Work

By the same token, teaching can help you in newspaper work, if you like this profession. Most teachers learn to write and think clearly and to recognize changes as they take place. Often a teacher makes a good copyeditor, because he or she is used to correcting mistakes.

Teachers & Writers Collaborative

Often one can combine his or her teaching and writing skills, such as in the Teachers & Writers Collaborative (T&W), based in New York City at 5 Union Square West, New York, New York 10003.

T&W publishes books about teaching writing and also houses the Center for Imaginative Writing.

The organization offers a limited program to sponsor performing and visual artists in schools. This gives artists and writers the opportunity to teach in various museum and arts programs around New York. To be considered for a residency through T&W, the professional writer or artist must have some teaching experience in the schools or in the community.

Sometimes a teacher holds a combination post—teaching full-time and holding a part-time newspaper job. Such an arrangement provides a source of added income. Often teachers can lend students practical experience in this way and learn of possible professional job opportunities for students. One professor at the Columbia School of Journalism is also music editor of a national magazine. This teacher encourages students to submit their work to different publications. An associate professor of journalism at George Washington University is also an assistant city editor at the *Washington Post*. He trains his students to have realistic goals with regard to their journalism careers.

Research Work

Many writers and publishing houses need research assistants to work on specific projects. This is a type of work that teachers can perform with competence. Research demands men and women who are well trained, who can express themselves clearly, and who can grasp the significant aspects of a subject without being told specifically what to do. Many teachers do research work for authors on special projects. This is a related field that should offer good future rewards.

Social Service Work

The social services offer many rewarding opportunities for those teachers who find work providing support services appealing.

Social and Community Work

There are various kinds of community work in which teachers may engage. Frequently the community center, the neighborhood social club, the adult education association, or the child study group in your city wants expert guidance from teachers. Many teachers serve as secretaries or part-time coordinators for these groups. Because of teachers' constant association with children, they are in a better position to know how to evaluate the needs of youngsters. Social, civic, and community work can be undertaken by members of the teaching profession to good advantage. Often the teacher combines his or her own job with that of a community worker in a related field.

Vocational Guidance Counseling

This field has grown tremendously during the past ten years, and it offers interested teachers many opportunities. More and more high schools have established guidance departments; some even include occupational courses in their curricula. Many boards of education offer their teachers in-service training in guidance. This field holds definite opportunities for those who are interested in helping students choose their careers and future education intelligently. Graduate counseling programs are accredited by the Council for Accreditation of Counseling and Related Educational Programs (CACREP).

Figure 5.1 Student Support Staff

Student Support Staff: Percentage of Regular Public Schools with Various Student Support Staff, by School Level: 1999–2000

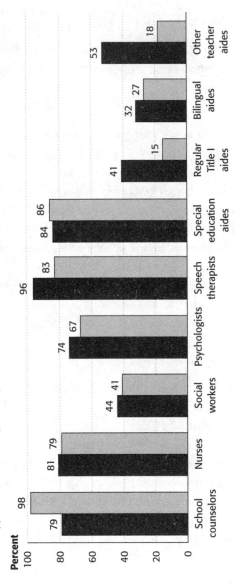

Percent

Legend:
■ Elementary ▨ Secondary

Elementary / Secondary values:
- School counselors: 79 / 98
- Nurses: 81 / 79
- Social workers: 44 / 41
- Psychologists: 74 / 67
- Speech therapists: 96 / 83
- Special education aides: 84 / 86
- Regular Title I aides: 41 / 15
- Bilingual aides: 32 / 27
- Other teacher aides: 53 / 18

Student support staff

Note: Data are for full- and part-time staff. Data for combined elementary and secondary schools and ungraded schools are excluded. Regular public schools do not include alternative, special education, special program emphasis, or vocational/technical schools.

Source: U.S. Department of Education, NCES, Schools and Staffing Survey (SASS) 1999–2000, *Public School Survey* and *Public Charter School Survey*.

Figure 5.1 shows the percentage of public schools that utilize the services of various support staff.

Counseling

In student personnel services, teachers may want to specialize in certain areas outside the classroom. An attendance officer, for example, is needed to check on students who fail to attend classes on a regular basis. The officer must cooperate with the rest of the personnel staff and attempt to identify causes and remedy the situation. Counselors and guidance directors in schools must interpret for the school community the changing needs of the students and help advise the students in various matters.

Other school positions that teachers may want to move into include psychologists, who help diagnose students' problems, and psychometricians, who administer, score, and interpret intelligence, aptitude, achievement, and psychological tests.

6

EDUCATIONAL ASSOCIATIONS

THE TERM "TEACHER POWER" is being heard more and more throughout the world. Teaching associations—leagues, unions, federations, clubs, and committees—have been in the public eye since strikes became common in the 1970s. Teachers, like doctors and other public servants, are no longer regarded as silent workers. Various educational associations help represent the teachers' interests. Involvement is a growing part of the role of the teacher in society.

Although teachers participated in a record 203 strikes during the 1975–76 school year, the 2002–03 school year saw a minimum of strikes—primarily due to the utilization of methods other than costly strikes to solve labor disputes. There has been an increase of special negotiation teams of teachers meeting with administrators.

Teacher organizations, such as the National Education Association (NEA) and the American Federation of Teachers (AFT), have included on their agendas issues like compulsory drug testing of probationary teachers, added retirement health plan packages, and the proposed major changes in teacher certification to represent teachers' interests.

Teacher Versus Administrator

Teachers are becoming increasingly aware of their rights and what laws protect their integrity in the classroom. In the case of Parducci v. Rutland (1970), the court agreed that a teacher had the academic freedom to use a book by Kurt Vonnegut that was not approved by school administrators because there was no evidence that the assignment was inappropriate or disruptive. Yet it is up to the teacher's sense of values to determine how far he or she can press individual rights.

One professor is critical of teachers' new outspokenness. In *The Fallacies of Academic Freedom and Professional Rights*, Robin McKoowan states that the rights issue will go too far in the future. "Educators may discover that teachers are employed primarily as experts to translate administratively designated district and school objectives into effective classroom programs and experiences," writes the author. "They may also discover teachers who decide not to teach required writing skills or social science inquiry strategies because 'there are better things to do.'"

History of Teacher Militancy

When a national teacher group formed in 1857, all "practical teachers" were asked to come to Philadelphia for the purpose of organizing a national teachers' association. The goals of the association, like those of state groups, were both to improve public education and teaching conditions and "to elevate the character and advance the interests of the profession of teaching, and to promote the cause of popular education in the United States."

Teacher groups did make gains before 1900, according to Marshall Donley in his book *Power to the Teacher*. Such acts as the establishment of kindergartens (1895), a constitutional mandate for free schools for all children (1870), and Illinois's first normal schools (1853–57) were promoted by the Illinois Education Association.

The New York State Teachers Association proposed a uniform system of licensing for teachers in 1887; a written licensing examination was instituted the next year. Before 1900, the New Jersey Teachers Association had started, in its words, "activities in the major fields that were to occupy it for the next quarter-century— retirement, tenure, and minimum salary—and growing out of them a vigorous program of legal defense of teachers whose rights as teachers were threatened."

The foundations of militancy were set early; teachers should have a say in the policy of the school. John Dewey said in 1903 that the public school system should be organized in such a way that every teacher has some regular and representative way in which he or she can register judgment upon matters of educational importance with the assurance that this judgment will somehow affect the school system.

Most teachers accepted the low pay, the low status, and the feelings that they could not correct injustices. But some groups showed signs of what would emerge in the future. A group of Illinois teachers won a salary victory in 1904. Despite bitter opposition by school directors, a minimum salary schedule was formulated. In 1908, a group of Virginia teachers pioneered a method that teachers now utilize—they held a mass rally in public to emphasize a cause. Teachers became more active in politics and school board elections.

One teacher strike that took place before World War I gained teachers in Memphis, Tennessee, a salary increase. Teachers won an additional ten dollars a month in wages.

Yet teacher militancy, as we now know it, only began to grow in the period after World War II, when the National Education Association organized teachers from across the country. Inflated prices after the war and added students and duties prompted the use of strikes. "Teachers all over the United States are thinking of striking," said progressive education leader George Counts. There were more than a hundred strikes from 1942 through 1959 carried out by different teacher groups.

Struggles Within the Organization

Although gains were constantly being made by teachers, most teachers were dissatisfied with their unions and associations. It was not until 1958 that the National Education Association (NEA) hired two salary consultants. Federal aid to education developed as a political issue when the Soviet Union launched the first spacecraft, Sputnik, into space. NEA leaders emphasized that higher salaries could attract more teachers in science and mathematics. The NEA currently is recruiting more members, in their words, "to add clout from the bargaining table to the halls of Congress."

The American Federation of Teachers is a labor union that represents teachers throughout the United States. Presently the AFT is known for its great militancy and increasing struggles with the NEA. Often the two associations fight with each other, causing fighting among teachers. A merger has been discussed between the two associations, but NEA refuses to join the AFL-CIO, which the AFT refuses to leave.

Teacher Rights

Over the years, teachers have become better informed about what legal rights they have. No longer prohibited from smoking or dancing, a teacher has complete say regarding what he or she does personally. In 1974, the Supreme Court struck down a widely enforced rule that required a pregnant woman to take a mandatory maternity leave, regardless of her ability to continue work. NEA President Helen Wise claimed the decision in favor of three teachers was "the greatest advance for female teachers since married teachers gained the right to teach." Former AFL-CIO president George Meany had defended public schools and public school teachers against their critics. Meany, addressing an AFT conference, pointed out that teachers who strike because of class-size increases were putting concern for the students first—something all too many elected officials neglect.

"The number of strikes in the public schools and other public services has been steadily rising simply because public administrators barricade themselves behind unfair laws that forbid public employees to strike or they seek court injunctions to keep teachers from exercising their rights as free men and women," commented Meany.

National Trends

Teachers must be aware of what their colleagues are doing around the country. Each decision regarding salary increase or size of classroom directly relates to all teachers. Joining teacher organizations and subscribing to journals and publications of the NEA, AFT, or other groups link one school with another.

"Teacher power" encompasses five basic causes of teacher militancy:

1. *Salary*—economic injustice
2. *Professionalism*—the larger meaning in a complex society

3. *Bureaucratization*—growth of schools
4. *Social climate*—changes within teacher groups
5. *Availability of mechanisms*—negotiation agreements and collective bargaining

Educational Associations and Organizations

Today there exist a number of associations relating to education and teachers' concerns.

National Education Association (NEA)

Acting as a parent body to thousands of local organizations, the National Education Association has its headquarters in Washington, D.C. The NEA keeps abreast of conditions affecting teachers. It prepares general policies and platforms for the profession as a whole and maintains a large research division.

Over the past few years, the NEA has won more and more bargaining influence with schools. Active in national politics, the association invests money in political activities. The NEA advocates adequate pay to retain promising instructors and steps to reduce classroom workloads. The organization acts as an aggressive watchdog to protect the jobs of teachers.

State Education Associations

There are statewide professional associations of teachers in every state, territory, and commonwealth in the United States. Their affiliations with the NEA permit them to send delegates to the NEA Representative Assembly, to receive various kinds of assistance from the NEA, and to cooperate closely in advancing education and the interests and goals of all professional teachers. To become affiliated with the NEA, a group must submit an application signed by 250 members of the association, representing at least twenty-five affiliates.

State associations include all kinds of educators in their membership. Many have active department programs. The annual conventions of many state associations are considered to be so valuable in the in-service education of teachers that schools are sometimes closed to allow teacher attendance.

Organizations Affiliated with the NEA

In addition to state educational associations, there is a wide variety of organizations working to improve the position of those in the education field. For instance, the NEA Higher Education Council was founded in 1974 and superseded the activities of several groups that previously benefited teachers of higher education. This organization works to improve the position of college teachers and administrators in the education workplace.

Membership in the National Council of Urban Education Associations is limited to associations of a thousand or more members whose organization is affiliated with the NEA. The council conducts two annual conferences and, according to its resolution, "seeks to act as a change agent in advocacy for teachers."

With headquarters in Switzerland, the World Confederation of Organizations of the Teaching Profession aims at gathering into one powerful organization teachers from all phases of education. With cooperation of international federations, some of its goals encompass promoting closer relationships among teachers in different countries, improving teaching methods and standards, and fostering a concept of education directed toward the promotion of international understanding and goodwill.

The American Association of School Administrators represents the principals, superintendents, and other administrators in the education profession. Its annual winter meeting attracts leading educators from all parts of the country. The association has helped make school administration a powerful factor in the campaign to improve teaching and provides a forum for innovative and excellent ideas for growth.

National Catholic Education Association (NCEA)

The NCEA is an organization representing all of the United States' Catholic school teachers—elementary, high school, seminary, and college level. This organization meets annually to discuss the various problems relevant to Catholic education. It publishes various pamphlets and reports dealing with Catholic education. Located in Washington, D.C., it is the central clearinghouse for information and data concerning Catholic education.

National Council for Accreditation of Teacher Education

The National Council for Accreditation of Teacher Education is a voluntary accrediting body made up of colleges and universities, state departments of education, school boards, teachers, and other professionals. They are devoted to the evaluation and accreditation of institutions for preparation of elementary and secondary teachers, school service personnel, and other school-oriented specialists.

United States Department of Education

The U.S. Department of Education cuts across all phases of education—elementary, secondary, college, public, private, and parochial—and acts as the clearinghouse for educational matters. Headed by the secretary of education, the office attempts to focus attention on the educational issues of the day. It serves to bring before the general public some of the major changes and developments that have taken place in American education. The secretary is appointed by the president of the United States and is also a member of the presidential cabinet.

National Council of Chief State School Officers

The National Council of Chief State School Officers draws together heads of the state school officials and gives greater prestige to the men and women working in education. It takes an active part in school problems and is thoroughly behind the movement to give more financial support to the schools of the country. It is an independent organization and is not affiliated with any other group.

American Council on Education

The American Council on Education speaks for all higher education, public and private. The council has brought together virtually all of the nation's colleges and universities and speaks with authority for American education. The newsletter *Higher Education and National Affairs* is published monthly by the council.

Council for Aid to Education

The Council for Aid to Education (CAE) is a not-for-profit private corporation that provides consulting and research services about voluntary support from corporations and information services to educational institutions regarding grants and private gifts. The results from the *Survey of Voluntary Support of Education* are published annually by the council. CAE has published a number of reports over the years on corporate giving trends as well as a "how-to" series, including guides on setting up matching gifts programs and guides on developing and managing corporate scholarship programs. CAE's report, *Intelligent Giving: Insights and Strategies for Higher Education Donors* (2002), provides a guide for prospective major donors in giving more effectively to higher education, and its annual Leaders for Change Awards program recognizes the best corporate-supported K–16 education reform initiatives. For more information contact Director of Research, Council for Aid to Education, 51 Madison Avenue, New York, New York 10010, or go to cae.org.

Council of State Directors of Programs for the Gifted

The Council of State Directors of Programs for the Gifted is composed of those in gifted education in each of the fifty states. The council conducts two comprehensive state surveys to produce a profile of gifted education throughout the United States. You can contact the Council of State Directors of Programs for the Gifted at Office of Public Instruction, P.O. Box 202501, Helena, Montana 59620. The website is nagc.org.

Council for Basic Education

The Council for Basic Education (CBE), located in Washington, D.C., was founded in 1956. Members receive the excellent *CBE Bulletin* and vote at annual or special meetings. There are many CBE publications giving information on the latest educational developments. The CBE is devoted to strengthening teaching and learning the basic subjects of school. For more information, Council for Basic Education can be contacted at 1319 F Street NW, Suite 900, Washington, D.C. 20004-1152, or go to c-b-e.org.

National School Volunteer Program

The National School Volunteer Program was established in 1964 with a Ford Foundation grant. There are an estimated two million volunteers who work with approximately five million children in some three thousand programs. The National School Volunteer Program says it seeks not only to "stimulate and aid the efforts of those engaged in school volunteer programs, but also to make the results of research and evaluation pertaining to educational volunteerism more readily available to educators, school volunteers, and teachers." Its monthly publication is *The School Volunteer.*

American Association of Colleges for Teacher Education

The American Association of Colleges for Teacher Education (AACTE) is a national, voluntary association of colleges and universities with undergraduate or graduate programs that prepare professional educators. The AACTE 750 member institutions make up 90 percent of new teachers' education institutions. In conjunction with the Lumina Foundation, grants for model teachers were awarded as a preparation initiative for Early Childhood Teaching programs at community colleges so students can transition to four-year-colleges. AACTE can be contacted at 1307 New York Avenue NW, Suite 300, Washington D.C. 20005-4701, or go to aacte.org.

For information on the "Preparing Future Faculty" program, contact the Association of American Colleges and Universities, 1818 R Street NW, Washington, D.C. 20009, or go to aacu-edu.org.

American Educational Studies Association

American Educational Studies Association (AESA) was established in 1968 as an international society for students, teachers, research scholars, and administrators who are interested in education foundations. AESA is a society primarily comprised of college and university professors who teach and research in the field of education utilizing a cross-disciplinary forum for comparative and international exchange.

Association for Career and Technical Education

The Association for Career and Technical Education is devoted to improving the quality of community college programs and developing high-tech vocational programs and computer training. For more information, contact the Association for Career and Technical Education at 1410 King Street, Alexandria, Virginia 22314, or go to acteonline.org.

American Association of University Women

A powerful advocate for women and girls since 1881, the American Association of University Women (AAUW) has helped create professional and training opportunities and promote academic excellence for women. The AAUW Educational Foundation funds graduate women and supports teachers and other programs. AAUW is located at 1111 Sixteenth Street NW, Washington, D.C. 20036, and its website is aauw.org.

American Association of Junior Colleges

Approximately 1,230 two-year institutions are represented by the American Association of Junior Colleges. To serve the diverse group of students enrolled in two-year institutions, an increasing number of faculty members and administrators are being employed at the junior college level. Usually the community colleges advocate an open policy of admission, stressing "excellence for everyone," according to the president of Miami-Dade (Florida) Community College. Since transfer from two-year to four-year colleges is becoming frequent, a number of states have taken steps to facilitate such transfers by regularizing standards and procedures.

The Eric Clearinghouse on Teacher Education

The Educational Resources Information Center (ERIC) is an organization that provides users with ready access to a wide variety of information on many subjects relating to education and teaching. Funded by the U.S. Department of Education's Office of Educational Research and Improvement, ERIC's Clearinghouse on Teacher Education (CTE) collects and stores information about teacher education. This information is retrievable electronically from most public or academic libraries around the country.

Association for International Practical Training (AIPT)

The AIPT is a private, nonprofit international exchange organization in Columbia, Maryland, that arranges and facilitates practical training opportunities for foreign nationals in the United States and American citizens seeking training abroad.

National Association for Women Deans, Administrators, and Counselors

This organization in Washington, D.C., offers counseling to women involved in higher education. The *Journal of NAWDAC* is a useful reference for all women in education.

Modern Language Association

Founded in 1883, there is a large membership of mostly college teachers of English and modern foreign languages in this association. Its basic purpose is to advance literary and linguistic studies in modern foreign languages, and the annual conference is a good opportunity to find out about teaching jobs in the field of language.

National Congress of Parents and Teachers

The National Congress of Parents and Teachers (PTA, formerly the Parent-Teacher Association) is a vitally important organization that brings parents and teachers closer together. It has state and local chapters throughout the country. In many communities, the PTA is the most powerful and most influential educational group in the area. The schools and the community are brought together within a working body through the efforts of the PTA.

The National Clearinghouse for Bilingual Education

This organization is funded by the U.S. Department of Education's Office of Bilingual Education and Minority Languages Affairs to collect, analyze, and disseminate information relating to the education of linguistically and culturally diverse learners in the United States. The George Washington University Center for the Study of Language and Education operates it. Those wanting to get more information or receive a list of the National Clearinghouse's publications can write to the National Clearinghouse for Bilingual Education Center for the Study of Language and Education, 2011 Eye Street NW, Suite 200, Washington, D.C. 20006 or go to ncbe.gwu.edu.

Unions

In addition to professional support, teachers can find employment opportunities in unions and other organizations if they wish to step out of the classroom. Chris Piluras, a professor of labor at the University of West Virginia, trains trade union people to do a better job. Starting first at a union local, he now works full-time for unions, educating teachers to better represent themselves.

American Federation of Teachers (AFT)

The AFT is considered more labor-oriented than the NEA, although many of its objectives are similar to those of the NEA. The major differences are in the pattern of organization, methods of achieving objectives, scope of program, and affiliation with organized labor. Under the presidency of Albert Shanker, the AFT rose in prominence by successfully negotiating its demands. The major means by which the AFT pursues its objectives are lobbying, collective bargaining, and strikes. About half of the total membership is concentrated in large cities.

The federation publishes a monthly newspaper, *American Teacher*, from its headquarters in Washington, D.C., and a quarterly journal entitled *American Educator*. The AFT supports a program called Universal Lifelong Education, which it initiated in 1974. The program calls for preschool education development, "second chance" education for working and retired citizens that encourages them to go back to school, and teacher training in the form of internships before a teacher starts work to see if he or she will adjust to the classroom.

Student Organizations

Future Teachers of America (FTA) was founded by the NEA in 1937 to help recruit teachers and to orient prospective teachers toward a better understanding of teaching as a profession. FTA programs provide information and experiences to help members decide whether they have the abilities and interests needed to become successful teachers. If there is no FTA club in your school and you are interested in forming one, write to the National Committee, FTA, 1201 Sixteenth Street, Washington, D.C. 20036. The American Federation of Teachers also has a future teacher organization, and it has student-teacher members in its local and state federations. Its stated aim includes the following:

1. To interest young men and women in teaching as a career
2. To provide its members with experiences to develop the qualities and aptitudes basic to successful teaching
3. To impart an understanding of the development and purpose of public schools
4. To aid in self-evaluation
5. To provide information and experiences that enable the student to explore and develop his/her vocation pursuant to a career in education

The Student National Education Association was founded in 1957 for college students preparing to teach. The Student NEA has approximately fifty thousand members in eleven hundred colleges and universities. Activities develop understanding of the teaching profession, preparation for teaching, and opportunities for involvement in politics. Student NEA members receive *Student Impact*, *Today's Education*, and other benefits and special services of the NEA.

Other student programs designed to help recruit, select, and orient teachers in specific fields such as music, business, and science are sponsored by subject area associations of teachers. Its website is nea.org/futureteachers.

Professional Fraternities, Sororities, and Societies

Several professional fraternities, sororities, and societies contribute to the advancement of the teaching profession as well as toward fellowship among teachers. Some publish journals and other publications, conduct professional programs, and stimulate research and discussion. Among the best known of the organizations are the following:

- Kappa Delta Pi is an honorary society that publishes the periodical *Education Forum*.
- Delta Kappa Gamma Society is one of the best-known women's organizations.
- National Society for the Study of Education is a small but influential group composed primarily of college professors. Its major activity is preparation of scholarly yearbooks.

Other Organizations

There are many other educational associations covering practically every aspect of the field. Many are oriented to special groups. Some of these independent national organizations include the Association for Childhood Educational International, American Association of University Professors, and the National Council of Teachers of English. Another organization is the nonprofit group Recruiting New Teachers (RNT). Founded in 1986 in Massachusetts, RNT is committed to encouraging students to pursue careers as educators. RNT's handbook, *How to Become a Teacher*, is available by calling (800) 45-TEACH or by checking its website at rnt.org. This organization also sponsors another Internet site that provides helpful information on becoming a teacher: recruitingteachers.org.

Teach for America is a program that helps students attain teaching jobs and maintain a stabilized salary and cost-of-living expenses. Since 1990, Teach for America has placed more than nine thousand college students across the United States, becoming one of the country's largest suppliers of teachers, according to the American Association of Colleges for Teacher Education. There are branches all over the United States with the headquarters at 315 West Thirty-Sixth Street, New York, New York 10018. The website is teach foramerica.org/tfa.

Programs for Community and Nonprofit Organizations

These government programs can provide special grants and other awards. Private schools can apply to the Center for Faith-Based and Community Initiatives, website ed.gov/faithandcommunity. Some of the program websites include:

Migrant Education-Even Start:
ed.gov/programs/mees/index.html
Early Reading First:
ed.gov/programs/earlyreading/index.html
Community Technology Centers:
ed.gov/fund/grant/applyadulted/ctc/index.html
Carol M. White Physical Education Program:
ed.gov/programs/whitephysed/index.html
Adult Education and Family Literacy State Grants:
ed.gov/fund/grant/find/adulted
Upward Bound: ed.gov/programs/trioupbound/index.html

Resources for Professional Development

For more information on programs sponsored by the U.S. Department of Education, call (800) USA-LEARN, or for program material on the Internet go to ed.gov.

Some other resources for professional development include the following:

American Association for Higher Education
One Dupont Circle, Suite 360
Washington, D.C. 20036-1110
(202) 293-6440, ext. 46
aahe.org

Association for Supervision and Curriculum Development
1250 North Pick Street
Alexandria, Virginia 22314
(703) 549-9110, ext. 312
ascd.org

California School Leadership Academy
313 West Winton Avenue, Suite 373
Hayward, California 94544
(510) 670-4563

Center for Collaborative Education
1573 Madison Avenue, Room 201
New York, New York 10029
(212) 348-7821
ccebos.org

Center for Research on the Context of Teaching
Center for Educational Research at Stanford
Stanford University
Stanford, California 94305-3084
(415) 723-4972
stanford.edu/gap/crc

Council for Professional Recognition
2460 Sixteenth Street NW
Washington, D.C. 20009-3575
cdacouncil.org

Far West Laboratory for Educational Research and Development
730 Harrison Street
San Francisco, California 94103
(415) 565-3000
wested.org

National Association for the Education of Young Children
1509 Sixteenth Street NW
Washington, D.C. 20036
naeyc.org

For information on teachers and the No Child Left Behind Act:

U.S. Department of Education
400 Maryland Avenue SW
Washington, D.C. 20202
ed.gov

7

MORE JOB OPPORTUNITIES
IN TEACHING

THOSE IN THE teaching profession need not be limited to the typical classroom. Many opportunities exist abroad, within various governmental and private organizations, and for specialized programs and purposes. Some of these opportunities are explored here.

Teaching Abroad

Teachers are in a unique position of qualifying for jobs almost anywhere they wish, anywhere that will help improve their positions. As the teaching job market in the United States has declined, the interest in opportunities for teaching abroad has grown. Salaries and benefits in other countries are not always equal to those in the United States, but often the experience is exciting. Scholarships, grants, and exchange programs are available to the teacher who wishes to teach in a foreign country. Yet teachers should carefully survey the field, for, as in the teaching profession in the United States, many job options are decreasing abroad.

A general minimum requirement for teaching positions abroad is a bachelor's degree and teaching certificate from a recognized U.S. college or university, although exceptions are sometimes made for unusually qualified personnel. Knowledge of the country's native language is not always required, but preference is often given to those candidates who possess such knowledge. The ability to teach more than one subject and a degree in Teaching English as a Foreign Language (TEFL) can be useful in obtaining a position.

Because appointments are made several months before the beginning of the academic year, investigations of overseas teaching opportunities should be made at least ten months before the beginning of the academic year in the foreign country. Appointments can often range from one to two years.

There are three major types of teaching overseas: government-sponsored, such as the Peace Corps or Teacher Exchange program; Department of Defense schools for dependents of military personnel overseas; and private schools, American schools, and other international schools.

It has become much easier to contact different programs, thanks in part to the Internet. One can go online to find which teaching job might provide a new vista and opportunity. A website like the one for the University of California, Irvine, Center for International Education, for example, utilizes resources in part with the United States Information Agency and NAFSA: Association of International Educators to offer international education opportunities. Go to cie.uci.edu to find out more. Some online services require an initial fee.

Government

The Teacher Exchange Branch, operated by the United States Information Agency, offers direct exchange of positions between U.S. teachers and foreign teachers. Another arrangement provides for one-way placement of U.S. teachers in schools abroad, such as in Germany and Denmark. The Teacher Exchange Branch annually publishes announcements of available opportunities and conducts a national competition for international teaching positions and seminar awards for American teachers. Teaching assignments are primarily open to elementary and secondary school teachers, college instructors, and assistant professors. Applicants must hold a B.A., be a U.S. citizen, and have at least three years' teaching experience.

Application procedures must be submitted by October 15 for the following summer or academic year's program. For information and applications, write to the Fulbright Teacher Exchange Branch, United States Information Agency, Washington, D.C. 20547.

Teaching opportunities are also available with the U.S. State Department. For further information, you can write to the Office of Overseas Schools, Room 234, SA-6, U.S. Department of State, Washington, D.C. 20520.

Peace Corps

Volunteers are recruited and trained to work as teachers in developing areas such as Africa, Asia, and Latin America through the federal agency known as the Peace Corps. Assignments are usually for two years, including a training period in the United States. Training, travel, and living expenses are paid. An allowance for every month spent overseas is paid to the volunteer in a lump sum at the end of service. Applications for Peace Corps positions are available from ACTION, Washington, D.C. 20525. ACTION is the agency that includes the Peace Corps, VISTA, the Foster Grandparent Program, and many other federally funded volunteer programs.

If you would like more information regarding government programs abroad, write for the booklet *Federal Jobs Overseas*, available from the Superintendent of Documents, U.S. Government Printing Office, Washington, D.C. 20402.

International Organizations

The United Nations Educational, Scientific, and Cultural Organization (UNESCO) looks for primary and secondary school teachers to work in underdeveloped countries. The Division of International Education, U.S. Department of Education, Washington, D.C. 20202, publishes a list of other international organizations that includes the name of the person in charge of employment for each organization.

Language and Area Study

The nonprofit Faculty Exchange Center (FEC), established in 1973, helps college professors exchange positions with colleagues in other regions of the United States as well as in foreign countries where English is the language of instruction. The program also facilitates "house exchanges" to encourage travel and study at all levels of the teaching profession. The FEC acts as a clearinghouse. To be listed in the FEC directory and for more information, write to FEC, 952 Virginia Avenue, Lancaster, Pennsylvania 17603.

Opportunities for teaching abroad are improved by the knowledge of teaching English as a foreign language. The organization Teachers of English to Speakers of Other Languages (TESOL) publishes a list of opportunities for those trained in the field. Most jobs listed require a master's degree and experience in teaching English as a second language. The list is available from 199 South Washington Street, Alexandria, Virginia 22314; tesol.org.

Defense

The largest employer of teachers working abroad is the U.S. Department of Defense. There are some 273 elementary, junior, and senior high schools in twenty-four countries for children of U.S. military and civilian personnel overseas. Teaching positions, as well as jobs as librarians, principals, administrators, and counselors, are available. Salaries are comparable to those in the United States. Assignments range from one to two years. According to the Department of Defense, applicants must "agree to accept an assignment throughout the world where a vacancy exists and where their services are needed." Information can be obtained at the Department of Defense, Overseas Dependent Schools, 2461 Eisenhower Avenue, Alexandria, Virginia 22331.

You can also write to the Defense Department for its booklet *Employment Opportunities for Education Overseas*, or contact the air force, army, and navy directly about teaching opportunities.

Private Agencies

There are many private agencies helping teachers locate jobs in other countries. Many schools are sponsored by corporations, like the Oil School in the Middle East. Company-sponsored school salaries are often low but include living expenses and other amenities.

The International Schools Service (ISS) recruits and recommends personnel for American schools abroad. The ISS operates a teacher placement bureau to locate elementary and secondary school staff for those schools attended by children of English-speaking business and diplomatic families abroad. Applicants must hold a B.A., be appropriately certified, and have two years of teaching experience. The ISS sponsors two national recruitments in the United States, with approximately 550 teaching and administrative positions available annually. For information on registration procedures, contact ISS, 126 Alexander Street, P.O. Box 5910, Princeton, New Jersey 08540.

The Institute of International Education has established a Register for International Service in Education (RISE) as a computer-based referral service to assist universities, government ministries, development projects, and other institutes outside the United States in locating staff for education-related assignments. These assignments may range from a few weeks to several years.

According to RISE, positions are open to those "qualified to teach, consult, or conduct research at the university or other post-secondary level; those qualified to teach trade and technical skills; and those qualified to teach English as a second language." U.S. citizenship is not required. For more information, you can write to RISE, Institute of International Education, 809 United Nations Plaza, New York, New York 10017.

Religious Organizations

Religious groups also recruit teachers for overseas schools. Teacher missionaries often started schools in foreign countries to introduce local inhabitants to Western religions and culture. The United Church Board for World Ministries refers and sometimes places candidates for teaching positions in high schools and colleges in

Turkey, Japan, India, and other countries. Assignments are generally for three years and are open to persons of all denominations as long as they have "the Christian motivation and concern." For information, you can contact the Personnel Secretary, United Church Board for World Ministries, 475 Riverside Drive, New York, New York 10027.

The YMCA Overseas Service Corps places young men and women as teachers of English. Preference is given to applicants with training or experience in linguistics or the teaching of English as a second language. Contact the Director, Overseas Personnel Programs, National Board of YMCAs, 291 Broadway, New York, New York 10007; ymcaiccp.org.

Some other places to write for information on teaching in religious schools abroad include the following:

Interboard Committee on Christian Vocations
Methodist Church
Nashville, TN 37202

International Liaison, Inc.
U.S. Catholic Coordinating Center for Lay Volunteer Ministries
1234 Massachusetts Ave. NW
Washington, DC 20005

Jewish Agency
515 Park Ave.
New York, NY 10022
(This agency assists those wishing to teach in Israel.)

Mennonite Central Committee
Personnel Services
21 S. Twelfth St.
Akron, PA 17501
mcc.org

Volunteers in Mission (VIM)
The Program Agency
The United Presbyterian Church
475 Riverside Dr.
New York, NY 10027
http://gbgm-umc.org/vim

United States Territories

Many school systems recruit and employ U.S. citizens for teaching positions in U.S. territories and outlying states. Here are some of the education departments:

Director of Education
Department of Education
Pago Pago
American Samoa 96920

Assistant Superintendent, Personnel
Department of Education
Government of Guam
Agana, Guam 96910

Secretary of Education
Department of Education
Hato Rey, Puerto Rico 00900

Foreign Governments and Placement Opportunities

The ministries of education of various countries are often excellent sources of information on current openings in their national school systems. Addresses of the ministries, which are usually located in capital cities, are available from the different countries' embassies or consular offices. Many countries recruit educators through their embassies in Washington, D.C.

Here is a partial list of places to write to, with groups divided into regions.

Latin America and the Caribbean

Accion
Box 27
Cambridge, MA 02138
(Volunteers on community development projects in Latin America)

Educational Personnel Services
Exxon Corporation
Charlotte Amalie
Department of Education
P.O. Box 630
St. Thomas, VI 00801
(Virgin Islands)

English Teaching Fellow Program
U.S. International Communication Agency
Washington, DC 20547

New York Employee Relations Office
1251 Avenue of the Americas
New York, NY 10020
(Aruba, Netherlands, Antilles, and Venezuela)

Asia

In the past few years, Asia, especially Japan, Thailand, and Taiwan, have been offering competitive salaries for teachers of English. With greater Asian interest in learning English, various schools have been developed. Salaries range in scale from twenty-five dollars per hour teaching private groups to basic monthly salaries.

Because many American companies have branches in Japan and other East Asian countries, job opportunities are often listed in English-language newspapers there. There are also some openings to teach content courses related to business topics in English. Some institutions are the following:

Asia Foundation
465 California St., 9th Fl.
San Francisco, CA 94104
asiafoundation.org

Association of Indian Universities
Rouse Ave.
New Delhi 110001 India
aiuweb.org
(Information on positions for U.S. teachers in India)

ECC (Thailand)
430/17-24 Chula 64
Siam Square, Paturnwan
Bangkok 10330 Thailand
(Teaching English and other classes in Thailand has become popular for Americans. One major teacher-training center can be located in Bangkok, and it has branches around Thailand.)

Embassy of the People's Republic of China
Cultural Counselor
2300 Connecticut Ave. NW
Washington, DC 20008
(All applicants for positions in China should include a detailed résumé indicating work experience and subjects they wish to teach in China.)

Foreign Affairs Department
Ministry of Education
Beijing, People's Republic of China
(For short-term teaching positions in English, foreign languages, science, and performing arts)

Foreign Experts Bureau
State Council
Beijing, People's Republic of China
(For two years or longer)

International Education Center
Japanese-American Conversation Institute
21 Yotsuya 1-chome, Shinjuku
Tokyo, Japan

Language Institute of Japan
4-14-1 Shiroyama, Odawarashi
Kanagawa-ken, Japan
geocities.com/lioj.geo

Reformed Church in America
475 Riverside Dr., Rm. 1818
New York, NY 10027
rca.org
(English teaching projects in Taiwan and Hong Kong for Christian-oriented singles younger than thirty years old)

Africa

Africa-America Institute
833 UN Plaza
New York, NY 10017
aaionline.org

African/American Educators Program
American Association of University Women
2401 Virginia Ave. NW
Washington, DC 20037
(Exchange of faculty)

International University Exchange Fund
P.O. Box 108
1211 Geneva 24, Switzerland
(Publishes educational opportunities in Africa)

Teachers for East Africa
Teachers College, Columbia University
New York, NY 10027

Middle East

American-Israel Cultural Foundation
4 E. Fifty-Fourth St.
New York, NY 10022
aicf.webnet.org

American University in Cairo
866 UN Plaza
New York, NY 10017
aucegypt.edu
(Two-year teaching fellowship for M.A. in teaching English as a
    foreign language)

International Institutional Services, Inc.
380 Madison Ave.
New York, NY 10017

Language Centre
P.O. Box 5486
University of Kuwait
Kuwait
kuniv.edu.kw
(For qualified TEFL-TESL teaching positions at the University of
  Kuwait)

Europe

Austrian Institute
11 E. Fifty-Second St.
New York, NY 10022

British American Educational Foundation
351 E. Seventy-Fourth St.
New York, NY 10021
baef.org
(A clearinghouse for independent school exchanges)

European Council of International Schools
19 Claremont Rd.
Surbiton, Surrey KT6 4QR
England
ecis.org
(Makes referrals with other schools and publishes an annual
  directory listing English-speaking international schools)

Italian Cultural Institute
686 Park Ave.
New York, NY 10021
italcultny.org

(Offers a booklet, *The Teaching of Foreign Languages in Italy*, and an occasional paper, "Employment Possibilities for American Teachers in Italy")

Near East/South Asia Council of Overseas Schools
Dr. Stanley Haas, Executive Director
American College of Greece
P.O. Box 60018
153-10 Aghia
Paraskevi, Greece
nesacenter.org
(Specializes in finding teaching positions in Greece)

Padagogische Austauschdienst
Sekretariat der Standigen Konferenz der Kultusminister der Lander
D5300 Bonn
Nasserstrasse 8
Germany

Australia and Pacific Territories

Associate Superintendent Personnel
P.O. Box DE
Agana, Guam 96910
(Teaching positions in Guam for secondary school teachers—special need in areas of science, math, and industrial arts)

Education Department of Western Australia
Parliament Place
West Perth, Western Australia 6005
eddept.wa.edu.au
(Positions in primary, secondary, and technical schools in Western Australia)

American Firms Operating Abroad

Some U.S. firms in other countries will accept a teacher's résumé directly if positions are open. Directories and lists of American firms and subsidiaries operating abroad, many of which are in the Middle East, are published by different presses offering specific information. You can write to one or more of the following:

Exxon Corporation
New York Employee Relations Office
Employment and Placement Section
1251 Avenue of the Americas
New York, NY 10020
exxon.com

Gulf Oil Corporation
2900 Gulf Bldg.
Pittsburgh, PA 15219

Sylvania Technical Systems Inc.
63 Second Ave.
Waltham, MA 02154

United Fruit Company
30 St. James Ave.
Boston, MA 02116

Agencies

Some of the following agencies request fees; others are paid by the school to hire teachers. Remember that many private organizations run summer school programs for high school students. Usually one teacher is needed to chaperone a group of about ten students.

Teachers can also organize a group to travel abroad. Some agencies with information include:

American Field Service (AFS)
313 E. Forty-Third St.
New York, NY 10017
afs.org
(Eight-week teacher exchange programs with Russia, Latin America, and East Asia)

The Experiment in International Living
Brattleboro, VT 05301
experiment.org
(For group leadership)

Friends of World Teaching
P.O. Box 1049
San Diego, CA 92112
fowt.com
(Supplies names for a fee)

International Camp Counselor Program/Abroad
National Board of YMCAs
291 Broadway
New York, NY 10007

International Schools
392 Fifth Ave.
New York, NY 10018

International Voluntary Services, Inc.
1717 Massachusetts Ave. NW
Washington, DC 20036

Scholarship and Grants

Many financial grants are awarded to study and teach in foreign universities. Often postdoctoral research is required. Teaching and studying in a school abroad is an exciting way to receive credit at the graduate level. Here are some sources of information on financial assistance:

American Institute of Indian Studies
Foster Hall, University of Chicago
1130 East Fifty-Ninth St.
Chicago, IL 60637
http://indiastudies.org
(Fellowships for study in India)

Association for International Practical Training
10400 Little Patuxent Parkway, Ste. 250
Columbia, MD 21044-3510
aipt.org

Fulbright Exchange Program
Department of State
Washington, DC 20005
(Check latest awards now available)
fulbrightexchanges.org

Institute of International Education
809 United Nations Plaza
New York, NY 10017
iie.org
(Offers annual brochure, *Grants for Graduate Study Abroad*, and
    other listings)

International Programs Office
201 Nolte West
315 Pillsbury Dr. SE
Minneapolis, MN 55455
(Financial awards directory)

Japan-English Fellows Program
CIEE
205 E. Forty-Second St.
New York, NY 10017
ciee.org
(School assistantships for those younger than twenty-five years old)

Rotary Foundation of Rotary International
1600 Ridge Ave.
Evanston, IL 60201
rotary.org

Study Abroad
UNESCO Publications
345 Park Ave. South
New York, NY 10010
http://upo.unesco.org/details.aspx?code_livre=4039
(Handbook on grants)

Publications

Many books and booklets can help you choose an overseas program according to your abilities. Some good sources include the following:

Educator's Passport to International Jobs
Peterson's Guides, Inc.
2000 Lennox Dr.
P.O. Box 67005
Lawrenceville, NJ 08648

Fellowships, Scholarships, and Related Opportunities in International
Education
The Division of International Education
University of Tennessee
Knoxville, TN 37916

International Jobs: Where They Are, How to Get Them
Addison-Wesley Publishers
2725 Sand Hill Rd.
Menlo Park, CA 94025

Overseas Opportunities for Teachers and Students
National Education Association
Office of International Relations
1201 Sixteenth St. NW
Washington, DC 20036

Schools Abroad of Interest to Americans
Porter Sargent Publishers, Inc.
11 Beacon St.
Boston, MA 02108
(Describes schools in 125 countries)

Study and Teaching Opportunities Abroad: Sources of Information about Overseas Study, Teaching, Work, and Travel
Superintendent of Documents
U.S. Government Printing Office
Washington, DC 20402

U.S. Non-Profit Organizations in Development Assistance Abroad
Technical Assistance Information Clearing House
200 Park Ave. South
New York, NY 10003

The World Trade Academy Press
50 E. Forty-Second St.
New York, NY 10017
(Publishes directories and lists of American firms abroad)

Teaching Opportunities in Canada

Canada, like the United States, is experiencing a shortage of teachers in certain rural and urban regions due to dramatic changes in the population, and this is creating an impact in teaching opportunities. There is no single system for education in Canada; the British North America Act of 1867 assigned responsibility for education to the provinces. Each province and territory has its own autonomous education system and thus makes decisions regarding schools, religious schools, private-school teachers, and curriculum.

There are approximately 310,000 teachers in the public elementary and secondary school systems of the provinces and territories and more than 84,000 teachers at work in community colleges, trade schools, universities, private schools, and band schools, according to the Canadian Teachers Federation. Teachers look for positions in Canada by applying directly to a particular school board or jurisdiction. To find listings of school boards, applicants should consult the website of the Ministry of Education for a specific province or territory—edu.gov.on.ca—or a local branch of the Canadian Teachers Federation.

Quebec and Ontario

"There is a demand for teachers due to retirement packages, economic strides from the recession, and an influx of immigrants in the booming provinces of Alberta and Calgary—both Canadian and foreign," said education career counselor Janice Tester of McGill University in Montreal, which has a special department in career guidance. "A new restriction in Quebec and Ontario is restructuring the schools along both religious and language lines, further requiring more teachers. In addition, students must now take two specialized subjects to qualify to become teachers."

Students can utilize the McGill University Career and Placement Service until two years after graduation. It is located in McGill's downtown Montreal campus at the Powell Student Services Building, 3637 Peel Street. Janice Tester also helps guide those who are not McGill students.

Qualifications for Teaching in Canada

Similar to the United States regulations, all beginning teachers in public elementary and secondary schools must have several years of university education in academic and professional subjects and usually hold a degree with one or two years in a teacher education program, except in certain vocational institutes. High school students preparing for a teaching career must hold qualifications suitable for entrance to a university degree program, since all teacher education in Canada now takes place in universities. The basic requirement to enter the teaching profession in most jurisdictions today is four years of postsecondary schooling with a grounding of both French and English. There are variations to this in some jurisdictions, and for more specific information candidates should contact relevant certification agencies such as: provincial/government tqs.edu.gov .on.ca.

The Canadian Teachers Federation advises, "Teaching is a life-long learning process and the initial preparation period is only a beginning. Emphasis is placed on continuing professional development, not only through formal graduate study at university, but also through short courses, workshops, travel programs, use of resource centers, and similar activities."

For those teachers who want to immigrate to Canada to seek employment in the public schools, all teacher requirements and qualifications must be submitted to the teacher certification body in the province or territory of application. Most provinces and territories require evidence of Landed Immigrant Status if the applicant is not a Canadian citizen. An important requirement for teachers coming from abroad is proficiency in one of Canada's official languages—English or French—although English is the major language of instruction outside of Quebec. Certain restrictions may affect some schools in various provinces due to policies, and employment authorization must be issued outside Canada before legally accepting a teaching job.

Networks

The Education Canada Network (http://educationcanada.com) has developed a website to assist job seekers. This site has teaching positions posted from the individual school districts/divisions across Canada. One of the popular features of the website is the Education Canada Résumé Registry, where visitors can post their own résumé. Teach Network (attn.org) is a "one-stop" recruitment center for teachers, school boards, and hiring principals, and Jobs in Education (jobsineducation.com) also assists job seekers.

Teacher Exchange Program

A variety of exchange programs are available to experienced teachers. Intraprovincial and interprovincial exchanges are frequently available through the departments of education. In addition, a number of provinces have made arrangements for exchanges with various countries, including Australia, Belgium, Bermuda, France, the Netherlands, Switzerland, and Germany.

The Canadian Education Exchange Foundation (ceef.ca) is a not-for-profit charitable organization committed to providing national and international exchange programs and services for students and educators.

Salaries

Salaries in Canada are comparable to those in the United States, although the Canadian dollar is lower in value. Teacher salary schedules in Canada are generally based on a combination of years of postsecondary education and years of experience, with additional allowances being paid to teachers with administrative responsibilities. The minimum salary for a teacher with one university degree, including teacher training (grade twelve plus four years postsecondary education), ranges from approximately $30,000 to $50,000 annually, depending upon the jurisdiction. In 2002, full-time university professors earned from $17,000 to $80,000, depending on their region.

Canadian Associations

There are various associations in Canada to approach about teaching opportunities. Teachers interested in obtaining university positions may consult the lists of vacancies published by the Association of Universities and Colleges of Canada, the Canadian Association of University Teachers, and Association of Canadian Community Colleges. Further information about private schools can be obtained by contacting the Canadian Independent Schools. To find out the latest information about the job market, contact the Canadian Teachers Federation or Human Resources Development Canada.

Canadian Teachers Federation
110 Argyle Ave.
Ottawa, ON
K2P 1B4
ctf-fce.ca

Human Resources Development Canada
Applied Research Branch
140 Promenade du Portage, Phase IV
Hull, QC
K1A OJ9
hrdc-drhc.gc.ca

Here are the federations around Canada:

The Alberta Teachers Association
11010-142 St.
Edmonton, AB
T5N 2R1
teachers.ab.ca

Association des enseignantes et des enseignants franco-ontariens
681, chemin Belfast
Ottawa, ON
K1G OZ4
http://franco.ca/aefo

Association des enseignantes et des enseignants francophones du
    Nouveau-Brunswick
C.P. 712
Fredericton, NB
E3B 5B4
aefnb.nb.ca

British Columbia Teachers Federation
100-550 W. Sixth Ave.
Vancouver, BC
V5Z 4P2
bctf.bc.ca

Elementary Teachers Federation of Ontario
1000-480 University Ave.
Toronto, ON
M5G lV2
etfo.on.ca

Federation of Nunavut Teachers
P.O. Box 2458
Iqaluit, NT
XOA OHO
fnt.nu.ca

The Manitoba Teachers Society
191 Harcourt St.
Winnipeg, MB
R3J 3H2
mbteach.org

New Brunswick Teachers Association
P.O. Box 752
Fredericton, NB
E3B 5G2
nbta.ca

New Brunswick Teachers Federation
P.O. Box 1535
Fredericton, NB
E3B 5G2
nbtf-fenb.nb.ca

Newfoundland and Labrador Teachers Association
3 Kenmount Rd.
St. John's, NF
A1B 1W1
nlta.nf.ca

Northwest Territories Teachers Association
5018-48 St.
P.O. Box 2340
Yellowknife, NT
X1A 2P7
nwtta.nt.ca

Nova Scotia Teachers Union
3106 Dutch Village Rd.
Halifax, NS
B3L 4L7
nstu.ca

The Ontario English Catholic Teachers Association
65 St. Clair Ave. East, Ste. 400
Toronto, ON
M4T 2Y8
oecta.on.ca

Ontario Secondary School Teachers Federation
60 Mobile Dr.
Toronto, ON
M4A 2P3
osstf.on.ca

Ontario Teachers Federation
1260 Bay St., Ste. 700
Toronto, ON
M5R 2B5
otffeo.on.ca

Prince Edward Island Teachers Federation
P.O. Box 6000
Charlottetown, PE
C1A 8B4
peitf.com

Quebec Provincial Association of Teachers
17035 Brunswick Blvd.
Kirkland, QC
H9H 5G6
qpat-apeq.qc.ca

The Saskatchewan Teachers Federation
2317 Arlington Ave.
Saskatoon, SK
S7J 2H8
stf.sk.ca

Yukon Teachers Association
2064 Second Ave.
Whitehorse, YT
Y1A 1A9
yta.yk.ca

Educational Links

Other links you can go to on the Web include:

Departments of education (OISE list):
    oise.utoronto.ca/~mpress/eduweb/ministries.html
Teacher organizations: ctf-fce.ca/en/aboutus/member.htm
Classification agencies: ctf-fce.ca/en/tic/appenc.htm
Faculties of education (OISE list):
    oise.utoronto.ca/~mpress/eduweb/faculties.html
Placement assistance agencies: ctf-fce.ca/en/tic/
    appene.htm
Canada-wide educational organizations (OISE list):
    oise.utoronto.ca/~mpress/canada.html

Human Resources Centre Canada:
hrsdc.gc.ca/en/home.shtml (These centers are located in
major urban areas. They are listed in the local telephone
directories.)
Private school placement: educationgroup.com
Canadian Association of Independent Schools: cais.ca
School boards: cdnsba.org

The *CEA Handbook* lists major school boards in Canada. It's
available from the Canadian Education Association, Suite 300, 317
Adelaide Street West, Toronto, Ontario M5V 1P9. Provincial lists
are available from the departments of education.

Other Opportunities

Federal and state governments, as well as other national organizations, offer various grants and awards for study and research. Different government awards aiding teachers change according to
budget. The National Endowment for the Humanities offers fellowships in residence for college teachers along with other programs. You can write for applications and the latest information to
the National Endowment for the Humanities, Washington, D.C.
20506.

Private endowments to colleges and universities are also increasing, many involving scholarships and funded study for students
committed to entering the teaching profession. Increased endowments by pharmaceutical companies and large industries are stressing the need for qualified teachers to teach these highly technical
subjects and to develop new discoveries for the twenty-first century.

More and more teachers are applying to private foundations for
grants to sponsor independent research and work on books and arti-

cles pertaining to their field of interest. Although funds are diminishing, grants—especially at the university level—are enabling teachers to take a break from the teaching routine and expand in their specialized areas.

Elementary schools, especially in economically distressed neighborhoods, have been receiving grants. Programs offer teachers new vistas to expand in teaching.

Project Head Start

Head Start, funded by the U.S. Department of Health and Human Services, is a nationwide project aimed at improving the educational experiences available to traditionally undereducated sections of the population. Head Start programs are offered at the kindergarten level through grade three, and many Head Start teachers have degrees in early childhood education. These programs have been very successful at introducing children to school and fostering an understanding of and commitment to formal education in the communities they serve.

Junior College Opportunities

Compared to other schools, teaching opportunities in junior colleges have been on the increase. According to a survey by the National Association of Independent Colleges and Universities, private colleges have recorded a decline in full-time enrollment, while part-time enrollment has increased. Two-year institutions—community, technical, and junior colleges—serve an estimated 4.5 million students. Many of the students are enrolled in vocational programs in occupational fields such as business, engineering technology, and health sciences. Although enrollment in these colleges has leveled off somewhat, there is still a need for qualified and committed faculty members in this area.

Sources of information about teaching positions in two-year colleges include the "Positions Open" section of the *Community and Junior College Journal,* published by the American Association of Community and Junior Colleges, One Dupont Circle, Washington, DC 20036; aacc.nche.edu. Check out also the Career Staffing Center, 621 Duke Street, Alexandria, Virginia 22314.

Continuous Growth

Programs to help teachers constantly improve in their fields are being conducted more and more often. Starting with teacher training, new innovations have helped to alleviate the feeling of stagnation that teachers often experience in their jobs. Often, too, new programs create jobs.

One experiment at a primary school in the Bronx, New York, introduced the teaching of health education in the curriculum. Students and teachers alike have expressed enthusiasm for the program, which has been viewed by educators here and abroad as a model for teaching health education. The curriculum has also created new positions for teaching health education at the primary level.

Teachers involved in other programs, such as the New York State Program for Excellence in Teaching, are being given monetary compensation for their skills in teaching. Prekindergarten and adult vocational and academic teachers are eligible to participate in the program, which has awarded $125 million annually.

As teachers are beginning to work together with their administration to formulate new programs, new avenues are being created to adjust to the rapidly changing society. Teachers play many different roles. "A teacher is a builder of the community," a "learner," and a "facer of reality," state Earl Pullias and James Young in the book *A Teacher Is Many Things*. A teacher is also "an actor; the center of attention for his audience at the moment," and a "scene designer," creating a scene in a vacant room. In this space, there is room for continuous growth.

Awareness of continuous growth is designed to keep the doors open for changing opportunities in the teaching field for the present and the future.

8

THE CHANGING ROLE OF THE TEACHER

As TECHNOLOGY BECOMES an increasingly important part of society, the teacher's role naturally must adapt to these changes. Because teachers are responsible for educating future generations, a teacher must be one step ahead of what is happening.

Technology

One of the first changes teachers must cope with, if they have been teaching in the school system for the past ten years, is the increased use of technology in the classroom. Teaching machines, educational television, computers, the Internet, and other devices such as interactive CD-ROM programs on computers, digital equipment, and videoconferencing, which are changing the concept of reading and writing by allowing the loading of whole texts, are frequently being used as teacher aides. As children grow up learning the alphabet from television programs such as "Sesame Street" and audiovisual machines become more and more an integral part of their education, an understanding of technology becomes essential for any teacher hoping to do his or her job well.

George Lucas, innovative filmmaker and creator of *Star Wars*, founded the George Lucas Foundation in 1991. Its aim is to focus on the advancement of teaching and learning through the application of innovative technology. The George Lucas Foundation develops interactive media applications for schools and homes, merging computer software with video, text, high-quality sound, and animation to teach a wide variety of subjects. The foundation has made an interactive video to be used in the classroom.

In 1960, Evelyn Solomon, a second-grade teacher at a Long Island, New York, elementary school, introduced an innovative program to her students. She used the radio to teach the students German. Each day the radio offered a new lesson in German. One former student said: "I learned German very quickly in that class. I remember sitting in the room, awed at an invisible voice instructing me in a foreign language. We all did well; children can pick up a language easily. How I wish other teachers had pursued this method of teaching later on in school. It seemed so penetrating and permanent at the time."

A basic skills program is different from programs focusing on development and creative thought. The latter involves self-analysis and personal growth. Thus, some educators believe that many forms of technology in learning will be dropped later on if there is no main purpose. For that reason, many people think that education will remain traditional with fixed standards. Today we see this idea manifested in a back-to-basics trend.

On the other hand, career education will require more use of vocational and technical materials in the school. Although the picture of a student plugged into a machine that is feeding him or her information appears too futuristic to some, perhaps in a few years, teachers will utilize learning machines in many situations. New jobs are created with the increased use of this equipment and sophisticated material.

"Television is the leading educator of today's youth," stated panelists at a Council for Basic Education conference. "Not instructional television (ITV), but out-of-school TV. Television's power as a teacher is well established."

Increasingly concerned about television's influence on young minds, the conference tried to contribute new ideas that would enable educators and those in the television industry to work together to enhance television's impact on learning in school.

Instead of fighting technology, we should use it to improve teaching and better prepare students to function in an increasingly computerized society, at least according to panelists in a video teleconference on microcomputers in education held at the University of Texas College of Education. Different participants, linked by telecommunications satellite, heard about the latest developments in microcomputer technology in education.

Most schools have incorporated use of the microcomputer in the classroom, and computer literacy is now an intrinsic part of modern education, often starting at the kindergarten level. New studies with the brain, computers, and technology are being conducted with an eye to the future and increased awareness of the information age. Despite added expense, technological education is proving increasingly important in the twenty-first century.

Technology will certainly be the focus as we gear up to meet the more sophisticated needs of the future. Interactive media and teaching will combine more often for an already-savvy student used to

TV channel surfing and high-tech entertainment. For example, at PBS Channel Thirteen's WNET Teacher Training Institute, teachers from throughout the New York tri-state region had a training program to learn to use technology and interactive methods such as video, online networks, and the Internet in the classroom. Such video-based lesson plans as "The Pressure Is On" helped teachers combine video, class participation, and hands-on experiments to demonstrate the properties of air pressure.

The PBS National Teacher Training Institute (NTTI), hosted by public television stations across the country, has grown from ten sites in 1991 to more than thirty in 2004. The institute is one of the nation's largest grassroots training programs in math and science for teachers. Locally recruited master teachers develop video and Internet-based lesson plans with classroom activities in various institutes to model strategies for combining technology with student and classroom participation.

Television learning can also bring conflict of interest with its advertising. North Salem High School environmental science teacher John Borowski said, "My school debated to renew its contract with Channel One, the media service that gives schools free television and cable access in exchange for its student audience, because at least 234 corporations supply the public schools with films, textbooks, and computer software—turning our children into the ultimate consumers."

Enrollment

The past decades have witnessed a trend to consolidate small schools, often bringing a large decline in the total number of public schools in the United States. For example, in 1930 there were more than 262,000 public schools, compared with around 88,000 in 1990. The number has grown in recent years.

Public school enrollment in kindergarten through grade eight rose 0.9 percent over fall 2001 to an estimated 47.78 million in fall 2002, according to NEA's report *Rankings and Estimates: Rankings of the States 2003 and Estimates of School Statistics 2004.* Private school enrollment for kindergarten through grade twelve increased from 4.7 million in 1989–90 to 5.1 million in 1999–2000. Between 1970 and 2002, the enrollment rate of twenty- and twenty-one-year-olds increased from 32 to 48 percent.

Digest of Education Statistics estimated that public elementary enrollment is expected to remain stable between 1998 to 2008, with public secondary school enrollment expected to rise by 11 percent. Public school enrollment is projected to set new records every year until 2006. Preprimary education enrollment had also grown substantially from 3.2 million in 1977 to 4 million in 1992 before decreasing to 3.7 million in 2001.

Undergraduate enrollment in the next ten years is projected to increase, according to the National Center for Education Statistics *The Condition of Education 2004* report. The numbers of part- and full-time students enrolled at two- and four-year institutions, with women's enrollment expected to increase faster than male undergraduates, are projected to reach a new high each year from 2004 to 2013. (See Table 8.1.)

These increases in enrollment coupled with anticipated increases in retirement rates will result in greater availability of teaching positions in higher education. This will enable nontenured faculty to move into tenured positions and will open the door further for newcomers to the field.

Changing Society

More than 40 percent of the children in the United States now live in single-parent homes, and the proportion of unmarried young

Table 8.1 Past and Projected Undergraduate Enrollments

Total Undergraduate Enrollment in Degree-Granting Two- and Four-Year Postsecondary Institutions (in Thousands), by Sex, Attendance Status, and Type of Institution, with Projections: Fall 1985–2013

Year	Total	Sex		Attendance Status		Type of Institution	
		Male	Female	Full-Time	Part-Time	4-Year	2-Year
1985	10,597	4,962	5,635	6,320	4,277	6,066	4,531
1986	10,798	5,018	5,780	6,352	4,446	6,118	4,680
1987	11,046	5,068	5,978	6,463	4,584	6,270	4,776
1988	11,317	5,138	6,179	6,642	4,674	6,442	4,875
1989	11,743	5,311	6,432	6,841	4,902	6,592	5,151
1990	11,959	5,380	6,579	6,976	4,983	6,719	5,240
1991	12,439	5,571	6,868	7,221	5,218	6,787	5,652
1992	12,538	5,583	6,955	7,244	5,293	6,815	5,722
1993	12,324	5,484	6,840	7,179	5,144	6,758	5,566
1994	12,263	5,422	6,840	7,169	5,094	6,733	5,530
1995	12,232	5,401	6,831	7,145	5,086	6,739	5,493
1996	12,327	5,421	6,906	7,299	5,028	6,764	5,563
1997	12,451	5,469	6,982	7,419	5,032	6,845	5,606
1998	12,437	5,446	6,991	7,539	4,898	6,948	5,489
1999	12,681	5,559	7,122	7,735	4,946	7,089	5,593
2000	13,155	5,778	7,377	7,923	5,232	7,207	5,948

2001	13,716	6,004	7,711	8,328	5,388	7,465	6,251
2002	13,829	6,008	7,821	8,438	5,392	7,705	6,124
2003	14,048	6,085	7,963	8,592	5,456	7,840	6,209

Projected*

2004	14,146	6,127	8,019	8,668	5,478	7,901	6,245
2005	14,329	6,183	8,146	8,797	5,532	8,011	6,318
2006	14,511	6,248	8,264	8,931	5,580	8,123	6,388
2007	14,634	6,304	8,331	9,033	5,602	8,201	6,433
2008	14,775	6,370	8,405	9,152	5,622	8,293	6,482
2009	14,965	6,448	8,517	9,298	5,667	8,414	6,551
2010	15,109	6,502	8,608	9,403	5,706	8,511	6,599
2011	15,255	6,547	8,708	9,493	5,762	8,600	6,655
2012	15,404	6,586	8,818	9,572	5,832	8,684	6,720
2013	15,568	6,622	8,946	9,657	5,911	8,771	6,797

* Projections based on data through 2000 and middle alternative assumptions concerning the economy.

Note: Detail may not sum to totals because of rounding. Data for 1999 were input using alternative procedures. See NCES 2003-060, pp. 509–12 for more information.

Source: National Center for Education Statistics, *The Condition of Education 2004.*

adults living with their families has declined from 90 percent in 1957 to about 50 percent today. The family as an institution is no longer the stabilizing factor it once was.

Such changes in the home environment influence how children adjust to school and reflect lower performance in the classroom, according to data from the Early Childhood Longitudinal Study. In 2001, 50 percent of children in kindergarten through grade eight were enrolled in a variety of nonparental care arrangements after school.

Educators urge that schools be prepared to deal with both legal and human concerns that may result from growing numbers of single-parent families. Single-parent homes also contribute to an increasing sense of isolation among youth, comments Harvey Greenburg, a specialist in adolescent psychiatry.

"Kids need a mentor or a patron," he says. "Teachers used to do this, but they do it less now because they're worn down, bitter, and paranoid."

A new trend is the Alternative Charter School. A survey found that one in four students do not attend a neighborhood school. Instead, they travel to other schools.

Violence

One of the most disturbing trends in school is the violence demonstrated by students against each other and against teachers in the classroom. Although statistics show that there is little increase from 1976 through 2003 of student victimization at school, according to a *Condition of Education* survey, there is an increasing pattern for students to use weapons and force resulting in loss of life. The school bully can be more dangerous in the guise of a frustrated student with a handgun.

A Columbia University study has found that school-based violence can be reduced at an early age. The two-year study (1997–99) of the Resolving Conflict Creatively Program, a pioneer violence-prevention program in New York City public schools, noted that students of these special classes proved to be less hostile and less likely to resort to aggression. In addition, academic achievement improved.

According to trends, teachers will be participating in more of these antiviolence programs around the country, which train not only students but parents as well.

There are programs such as Community Partnerships, which promotes family involvement with the schools; Twenty-First Century Community Learning Centers, which are funded by the U.S. Department of Education to provide after-school and summer learning centers; and various programs promoting safe and drug-free school environments.

Back to Basics

Concern for declines in standardized test scores and quality of education has prompted a back-to-basics movement in education. Although some professors complain that their students lack basic knowledge previously taught at an earlier level, learning in the age of technology is being reexamined to plug any noticeable gaps. When the National Assessment of Educational Progress (NAEP) conducted a test for eight thousand public and private high school juniors about basic history and facts, more than 64.5 percent of the students failed, showing lack of common knowledge.

Students are not reading and writing to correct levels—only one-quarter of American students can write at proficient levels, according to various reports. These statistics have worried educators.

During the first part of the twenty-first century, more than ever the reading and writing abilities of students will be the most important factor to deal with complex issues and evolving technology of the future.

Teaching with New Techniques

Teaching techniques have created new methods to interest students in learning. One imaginative method is called "Reacting to the Past," where the classroom turns into a reenactment of past events with performance and student recitations. At a Reacting to the Past seminar held in June 2004 at Barnard College in New York City, more than fifty faculty members and administrators from eighteen institutes attended its fourth conference to discuss new forms of outreach to students and how to increase their enthusiasm in all subjects, especially history. An estimated one hundred faculty members at two dozen institutions use these innovative teaching methods, which are also promoted by the Department of Education's Fund for the Improvement of Post-Secondary Education.

"We hope that kind of breakthrough might help renew our fractured world by enabling students to understand other times and societies," said Barnard College president Judith Shapiro, where its history project won the Hesburgh Award as outstanding new model of undergraduate teaching and learning.

Service Teaching

Teachers are beginning to combine academics with social responsibility and a "how to" approach to learning in a program called Service Teaching.

"The East Bay Conservation Program in Oakland has shifted the emphasis outside the classroom and has put thinking into the curriculum for the students," says Marianne Ellis, a former teacher and principal in the Oakland, California, school district. Ellis now helps develop Service Teaching programs. "We don't want our students just listening to a teacher or being put in front of a computer or a television. We utilize the 'how to' approach, bringing students to the parks to learn science, learning how to make a quilt, and making the most of having the kids teach the kids."

Involving the Community

Education must seek involvement with the community due to an aging population and more families that are childless, recommend educators.

The message for the future of education, according to numerous reports and studies, is "back to basics" for both student and teacher. A focus on the core curriculum is being urged by Allan Bloom in his best-selling book *The Closing of the American Mind: How Higher Education Has Failed Democracy and Impoverished the Souls of Today's Students* to prevent the danger of students "closing their minds" to basic knowledge. The teacher is being advised to return to the "basic teaching skill." "Nobody flunks a museum," said Frank Oppenheimer, founder of the San Francisco Exploratorium, which is involved in bringing students into museums, where teachers can have a broader forum for the science classes.

Teachers have been given added responsibility in educating students about the dangers of drugs and sexually transmitted diseases like AIDS and helping those who are at risk of alcohol abuse and suicide. The United Teachers program Helping Children at Risk helps train teachers in this relevant health-sensitive area. Teachers are working together with the community to combat the social problems that today's youth are facing.

"In my own studies of successful schools, I had concluded that the most efficient and effective ones create and sustain a sense of community," writes Rexford Brown in his book *It's Your Fault: An Insider's Guide to Learning and Teaching in City Schools*.

Educating the Community

"When I first started teaching, I figured that if my kids could survive me, they could make it anywhere," said Joe Marshall, a San Francisco teacher who won a 1994 MacArthur Fellowship for founding the Omega Boys Club for inner-city San Francisco African-American youths. "But I found that my own students, who were bright, would be writing to me from prison or while on drugs. That's when I knew I had to extend myself beyond the classroom."

Marshall's efforts in promoting the Omega Boys Club as an alternative place to study and prepare for college has resulted in many of the students enrolling in colleges and universities. Teachers such as Joe Marshall have realized that students sometimes need more education than what is offered in the classroom setting. This is a project that requires the work of many committed and trained adults working together for the good of the students. The Urban Teacher Academy Project (UTAP) is a collaborative effort of Recruiting New Teachers, Inc. (rnt.org) and the Council of the Great City Schools (cgcs.org) to promote the recruitment and preparation of qualified and diverse teachers for urban schools by establishing high school teaching career academies. Various profiles of the teaching academies from Miami Senior High School to Walton High School in New York City can be found in the booklet

High School Teaching Career Academies: Profiles and Practices to inspire future teachers.

Gifts to Help Teachers

When William Gates, chairman of the Microsoft Corporation, announced a gift of $1 billion in college scholarships to deserving minority high school seniors over the next twenty years, he joined a trend of big business groups participating in the nation's education process.

"I think the national community has realized it isn't enough just to give to higher education," stated Eugene Lang, who adopted fifty-four sixth-graders at a Harlem school in 1981 and committed to send them to college. "You've got to catch children before they fall into that abyss."

In 1998, Wall Street financier Theodore Forstmann gave $100 million to help forty thousand inner-city public school students attend private schools; and the Milken Family Foundation awarded $40 million in $25,000 grants to 172 elementary and secondary school teachers. In 2003, billions of dollars were donated to help schools. The teacher of the future will be well aware of the resources at hand and try to better utilize these funds.

This trend marks an exciting development for the teacher. It shows that the business community believes that a good education is the cornerstone of a successful nation.

Teacher Honors

There are several incentives to become a teacher, and one is to receive special honors. The *USA TODAY* newspaper honors annually twenty teachers from kindergarten through grade twelve as outstanding educators and names them to the All-Stars-USA Teacher Team. A cash prize of $2,500 ($500 to the teacher and the rest to the school) is given. Teachers may be nominated by anyone who writes how the "teacher has unlocked students' minds and made a difference in their lives." The website is: allstars.usatoday.com.

Teaching Ethics

As moral codes have changed in recent times, many educators are being urged to take responsibility and re-instill values in the classroom by teaching the relatively new and old subject of ethics. One result of ethics dilemmas in the business world was a $20 million endowment by former Securities and Exchange Commission Chairman John S. R. Shad to establish a business leadership and ethics program at the Harvard Business School in 1987. It also raises the question of whether business professors or philosophy professors should teach ethics. "There is a major decision to be made up-front in teaching ethics," says Kirk Hanson, who taught a course called "Ethical Dilemmas in Management" at Stanford University. "Do you try to convince students to have ethics? Or do you help them clarify their values and carry them out consistently? We help students build an awareness of where ethical issues arise."

The American Council on Education has recommended improving curriculum offerings in traditional courses in philosophy, religion, literature, and political science as well as creating new courses in moral reasoning and professional ethics.

Women

Although women are receiving greater opportunities in some fields, teaching still remains one of the most competitive areas for a woman. Primary and secondary positions customarily filled by women are becoming increasingly scarce. Fields such as engineering, law, and business, however, present a better picture. Statistics show that women are opting to major in these subjects in far greater numbers than they had a decade earlier.

Yet enrollment patterns show that a majority of women major in those areas where employment opportunities are diminishing, including education, fine arts, foreign languages, psychology, and letters. In the tight job market, unless they also possess marketable skills such as accounting, computer sciences, statistics, or personnel administration, many women will have difficulties in obtaining employment.

Women have increasingly become involved in the field of women's studies, which has opened new opportunities for teachers to hold positions in colleges and contributed to more teaching jobs specifically for women. Several women's organizations advocate more faculty positions for women in higher education, thereby promoting awareness of women in the field of education.

There are also more opportunities for women to receive scholarships to universities in sports programs. It has been estimated that more than ten thousand young women can attend college on athletic scholarships a year. Teaching sports in schools has also increased. The American Association of University Women is a good starting point to find out which scholarships and funds are available for interested young women.

Ethnic Groups

Teaching ethnic courses for Indians, Chinese-Americans, African-Americans, Latinos, and other minorities is becoming a specialty of teachers for the future. In Miami, Florida, most schools are becoming bilingual, and teachers are beginning to teach Cuban history and subjects relevant to the student body.

The Latino community is growing so fast that some say that within the next few years there will be a Latino majority in some cities. There has even been a White House Initiative on Education Excellence for Hispanic Americans; contact yesican.gov. When disadvantaged students enter college, they often lack certain basic skills, especially in mathematics and science. The problem has been combated with instructional methods tailored to fit the needs of a particular student.

Alabama's Miles College is an "open door" college that bases candidate admissions not on test scores but on careful evaluation of each individual's potential. The Miles biology program features audio-tutorial instruction divided into minicourses consisting of films, slides, tape recordings, demonstrations, and short reading assignments. Individual instruction in subjects such as chemistry and mathematics has helped many of the students overcome difficulties.

Basic reading skills are stressed by educators to help students learn how to absorb what they will be taught in the future. A sound knowledge of grammar, sentence structure, and interpretation cannot be easily forgotten.

Tutors can be a great help to students, especially those from disadvantaged areas. For example, a tutorial assistance program was set up at the University of Texas to help students find someone who will counsel or teach them in a study skill. Courses in mathematics and science are used by an estimated ten thousand students per year. Student teachers who would like to see how they relate to a student can receive both practical and emotional experience from this tutorial teaching.

Educators are stressing the role of largely African-American colleges and universities in producing an adequate supply of African-American teachers. Groups like the National Congress of Black Faculty recruit and retain African-American faculty members. Endowments, like the $25 million John Kluge scholarship for minority students at Columbia University, encourage higher education, while some universities, such as Syracuse in Ohio and the University of Texas, have established special programs to guarantee admission of selected minority students in the public school system into their universities.

The National Center for Education Statistics found out that relatively fewer minorities were in the teaching force than in the population they served. As schools and colleges become aware of the importance of ethnic teaching due to the growing number of minorities now born in the United States, education will increasingly be shaped to meet the needs of the emerging multicultural society. Teaching will be an important factor in educating those from other cultures about the American way of life with a challenging core curriculum that helps them blend into the mainstream while providing them with a good education. Teachers must be able to recognize and respond to individual and cultural differences in students and employ different teaching methods that will result in higher student achievement.

Professional Development

Many states now offer professional development schools—partnerships between universities and elementary or secondary schools. Students enter these one-year programs after completion of their bachelor's degree. Professional development schools combine theory with practice and allow the student to experience a year of teaching under professional guidance.

Job Market

The changing role of the teacher and declining enrollments are reflected in the changing job market. As a future teacher, you must be aware of an often-shrinking demand for teachers. Reading material with a critical eye, you must keep up-to-date on the competition, government cutbacks, and other hazards of the teaching profession. New inroads to becoming a teacher must be developed.

Job opportunities for teachers over the next ten years will vary from good to excellent, depending on the locality, grade level, and subject taught, according to the U.S. Department of Labor. Most job openings will be attributed to the expected retirement of a large number of teachers. In addition, relatively high rates of turnover, especially among beginning teachers employed in poor, urban schools, also will lead to numerous job openings for teachers. Competition for qualified teachers among some localities will likely continue, with schools luring teachers from other states and districts with bonuses and higher pay. Through 2012, overall student enrollments, a key factor in the demand for teachers, are expected to rise more slowly than in the past. The job market for teachers also continues to vary by school location and by subject taught (see Table 8.2).

A Strong Profession

The teaching profession is strong. It has substantial support from all who believe in the American way of life and from all who recognize that education is a mainstay of democratic society. When-

Table 8.2 Estimated Number of Instructional Staff Members in Public Elementary and Secondary Schools by Type of Position, 2003–04

| Region and State | Classroom Teachers | | Total Teachers | Other Non-Supervisory Instructional | Principals & Supervisors | Total Instructional Staff |
	Elementary School	Secondary School				
50 states & D.C.	**1,764,977**	**1,286,753**	**3,051,731**	**232,944**	**184,258**	**3,468,933**
New England	**97,237**	**74,497**	**171,735**	**20,943**	**8,866**	**201,543**
Connecticut	30,482	12,767	43,249	4,579	2,675	50,503
Maine	11,070	5,135	16,205	1,397	1,138	18,740
Massachusetts	31,888	42,284	74,172	9,800	3,500	87,472
New Hampshire	10,800	4,679	15,479	2,212	755	18,445
Rhode Island	8,333	5,331	13,664	1,993	366	16,023
Vermont	4,664	4,302	8,966	962	432	10,360
Mid-Eastern	**258,171**	**266,096**	**524,267**	**47,732**	**26,950**	**598,949**
Delaware	5,448	2,341	7,789	606	484	8,879
District of Columbia	2,634	1,044	3,678	971	326	4,975
Maryland	34,347	22,337	56,684	5,117	3,683	65,484
New Jersey	40,242	67,174	107,416	16,238	6,557	130,211
New York	113,000	115,000	228,000	12,000	10,000	250,000
Pennsylvania	62,500	58,200	120,700	12,800	5,900	139,400

(continued)

Region and State	Classroom Teachers			Other Non-Supervisory Instructional	Principals & Supervisors	Total Instructional Staff
	Elementary School	Secondary School	Total Teachers			
Southeastern	**453,452**	**296,949**	**750,400**	**59,382**	**47,692**	**857,474**
Alabama	27,795	19,435	47,231	4,000	2,858	54,089
Arkansas	15,986	16,633	32,619	2,753	2,097	37,468
Florida	71,566	72,029	143,595	9,136	7,021	159,752
Georgia	56,158	40,794	96,952	8,395	6,939	112,286
Kentucky	25,897	11,054	36,951	4,890	1,911	43,752
Louisiana	35,344	15,331	50,675	4,848	3,797	59,319
Mississippi	18,285	12,407	30,692	1,940	2,091	34,723
North Carolina	55,560	32,385	87,945	6,491	5,663	100,100
South Carolina	33,023	12,829	45,852	3,858	4,252	53,961
Tennessee	43,494	16,430	59,924	4,540	3,873	68,337
Virginia	56,617	41,480	98,097	7,292	5,701	111,090
West Virginia	13,727	6,142	19,869	1,239	1,489	22,597
Great Lakes	**265,302**	**177,260**	**442,562**	**30,306**	**27,765**	**500,633**
Illinois	91,318	44,496	135,814	5,473	7,573	148,860
Indiana	32,177	28,384	60,561	3,000	4,727	68,288
Michigan	15,912	44,458	60,370	8,973	6,268	75,611
Ohio	83,713	41,066	124,779	8,900	6,600	140,279
Wisconsin	42,182	18,856	61,038	3,960	2,597	67,595
Plains	**117,300**	**104,718**	**222,018**	**14,247**	**12,746**	**249,011**
Iowa	16,486	18,298	34,784	2,377	1,372	38,533
Kansas	16,025	16,563	32,588	2,581	2,174	37,343

Minnesota	26,553	25,686	52,239	2,023	2,773	57,035
Missouri	33,211	31,830	65,041	4,177	4,397	73,615
Nebraska	13,525	7,148	20,673	1,764	1,250	23,687
North Dakota	5,178	2,484	7,662	810	384	8,856
South Dakota	6,322	2,709	9,031	515	396	9,942
Southwestern	**216,739**	**184,519**	**401,258**	**27,595**	**25,154**	**454,008**
Arizona	30,821	14,711	45,532	4,176	3,108	52,817
New Mexico	15,030	6,445	21,475	2,909	1,015	25,399
Oklahoma	20,365	18,718	39,083	2,820	2,456	44,359
Texas	150,523	144,645	295,168	17,690	18,575	331,433
Rocky Mountains	**52,685**	**47,084**	**99,769**	**7,521**	**6,161**	**113,451**
Colorado	23,650	23,217	46,867	3,546	2,787	53,200
Idaho	7,169	6,902	14,071	782	1,030	15,882
Montana	6,857	3,441	10,298	947	498	11,743
Utah	11,950	10,124	22,073	1,729	1,516	25,318
Wyoming	3,060	3,400	6,460	518	330	7,308
Far-Western	**304,091**	**135,631**	**439,722**	**25,217**	**28,925**	**493,864**
Alaska	5,204	2,796	8,000	451	468	8,919
California	234,001	85,913	319,914	15,919	20,706	356,539
Hawaii	6,007	5,255	11,262	1,989	516	13,767
Nevada	11,849	8,196	20,045	2,204	1,047	23,296
Oregon	17,780	9,888	27,668	1,378	2,674	31,720
Washington	29,250	23,583	52,833	3,276	3,514	59,623

Source: National Education Association, *Rankings & Estimates: Rankings of the States 2003 and Estimates of School Statistics 2004*, May 2004.

ever a crisis has appeared, teachers have been on hand to help both the government and organizations needing advice and counsel.

Many educators, troubled by the motivation of students, are looking at Japanese schools as role models instilling the inspiration to make a nation economically and morally strong. When German educator Friedrich Froebel founded the first kindergarten in 1840, his intention was to provide a "garden for children," where the young would grow up protected and looked after like plants in a garden.

As preprimary and kindergarten schools increase, the education of the young will become an important responsibility of the teacher. The "flowers" of the garden can be either crushed or allowed to bloom.

The role of the teacher in society is growing stronger in importance. New methods of education offer new challenges and new opportunities for the teacher. The prophet who said "seek and you shall find" could have been referring to searching for the job you really want. There is no profession finer than that of a teacher. In the words of a poet:

Would you set your names upon the stars?
Then write it large upon the hearts of children.
They will remember.
Have you visions of a finer, happier world?
Tell the children.
They will build it for you.

Further Information

ALTHOUGH WE HAVE tried in this book to be as comprehensive as possible regarding the opportunities open to those interested in teaching, there are many other sources of information that can provide valuable assistance to prospective teachers.

Periodicals

The American School Board Journal
800 State National Bank Plaza
Evanston, IL 60201

Bulletin
National/State Leadership Training Institute on the Gifted and
    Talented
316 W. Second St.
Los Angeles, CA 90012

Council on Basic Education (CBE) Bulletin
725 Fifteenth St. NW
Washington, DC 20005
(Includes job listings and new trends)

The Educational Forum
Kappa Delta Pi
West Lafayette, IN 47906

Forum
National Clearinghouse for Bilingual Education
1300 Wilson Blvd.
Rosslyn, VA 22209

Higher Education and National Affairs
American Council on Education
One Dupont Circle
Washington, DC 20036

Language Arts
National Council of Teachers of English
1111 Kenyon Rd.
Urbana, IL 61801

Memo: American Association of State Colleges and Universities
American Council on Education
One Dupont Circle
Washington, DC 20036

NEA Today
National Education Association
1201 Sixteenth St.
Washington, DC 20036

Network
National Committee for Citizens in Education, Ste. 410
Wilde Lake Village Green
Columbus, MD 21044

Newsbrief
Association for Children with Learning Disabilities
4156 Library Rd.
Pittsburgh, PA 15234

Resources for Youth
National Commission on Resources for Youth, Inc.
605 Commonwealth Ave.
Boston, MA 02215

Teaching's Next Generation: A National Study of Precollegiate Teaching Recruitment
Recruiting New Teachers, Inc.
385 Concord Ave.
Belmont, MA 02178

Books and Directories

Brown, Rexford. *It's Your Fault: An Insider's Guide to Learning and Teaching in City Schools.* New York: Teachers College Press, 2003.

Bureau of Labor Statistics. *Occupational Outlook Handbook 2004–05.* New York: McGraw-Hill.

Cahn, Steve. *Classic and Contemporary Readings in the Philosophy of Education.* New York: McGraw Hill, 1996.

Clinch, Evans. *How Small Schools Are Changing American Education.* New York: Teachers College Press, 2000.

Goodlad, John, and Timothy McMannon. *The Teaching Career.* New York: Teachers College Press, 2004.

Montessori, Maria. *The Absorbent Mind.* New York: Owl Books, 1995.

National Education Association. *Rankings and Estimates: Rankings of the States 2003 and Estimates of School Statistics 2004.* Washington D.C.: NEA Research, 2004.

Palmer, Peter. *The Courage to Teach: Exploring the Inner Landscape of a Teacher's Life.* San Francisco: Jossey-Bass, 1998.

U.S. Department of Education. *The Condition of Education 2004.* Washington D.C.: National Center for Education Statistics, 2004.

U.S. Department of Education. *No Child Left Behind: A Tool Kit for Teachers.* Jessup, Md.: U.S. Department of Education, 2004.

U.S. Department of Education. *What to Expect Your First Year of Teaching.* Washington D.C.: U.S. Department of Education, 1998.